This.

By Kristen Cook

Dedication

For Nos. 1, 2 and 3. You know who you are. I hope. I love you all more than anything and know that when I yell at you for being pigs, it's only because I really, truly want you to not be so messy. Now, go clean up your rooms.

Oh K/Cathy, my K/Cathy… My beloved friends and same-named coworkers. Thank you for the belly laughs — and snorts — of validation and your endless support.

For Jenni and Sharon, my fashion friends, my confidantes, my sisters. I would be lost without you.

For Sherry, who always told me to write a book. Hey, I listened!

For Mike and Helen, you give in-laws a good name.

For my little bro Alan, Albutt, Albagoonda, thanks for letting me be the boss of you.

For Adrienne, Myles, Tom, Joel and Henry, thanks for the help and advice.

For my parents whose emotional and financial support made this whole thing possible (Whoa! Kinda makes them sound like NPR sponsors, which in truth, they are).

For Joe, my soulmate, father of my children, my tireless supporter, willing butt of my jokes, I do hereby officially forgive you for that time you grabbed the video camera and recorded me in night-vision mode, as I snored away, and proceeded to mock me while pretending you were "The Crocodile Hunter" happening upon some strange, loud beast.

And, for every person who ever complimented me on my shoes, I love you.

"Never, never, never give up."

Winston Churchill

"If I cannot do great things, I can do small things in a great way."

Martin Luther King, Jr.

"You don't regret the things in life you do, you regret the things you don't do."

My husband, and apparently also Hugh Jackman and Hugh Laurie in a 2012 Facebook post.

"Yippie kayak, other buckets."

Charles Boyle, "Brooklyn 99" (Season 3, Episode 10)

Table of Contents

Why I Wrote *This*.

You may not have heard of me (Kristen Cook), but this is actually my fifth book. That is, if you count the *fauxmance* novellas I wrote my college besties for their birthdays featuring them plus their crushes du jour and if you consider the children's books intended to shame one of my kids into bathing and to get another to read something, anything, other than "Tiny Titans."

But, those weren't published.

Unless it counts to print them out and have AlphaGraphics laminate and bind them. And, quite frankly, I think it does because that is what you call OG self-publishing, my friends.

So…why did I write *This*.?

Well, here's the thing: I had been writing a newspaper column called Minivan Momologues, mostly goofing on everyday family stuff, when the plug got pulled. The paper was shrinking yet again and while I cannot do a thing about my hips no matter how hard I exercise, this managerial move lopped off a sizeable piece of my heart. I missed writing that column. Realized I wasn't finished just yet. I found myself at a reporting job that I didn't really like any more at the same time my oldest child was visiting colleges — expensive ones that cost twice what I made in a year. It made me wonder why I continued to stay at a job I no longer loved and that paid less than a fast-food joint. Plus, I envied how the world was full of possibilities for her. I wanted that, the excitement and thrill of new challenges, and so maybe, for once in my life, I needed to take a chance and make like a Nike ad, only a mere 29 years after its groundbreaking campaign and…Just Do It. Maybe I should just quit and do what every person who's ever had a byline has dreamed about — write a book.

That was already bouncing around in my head when I was sitting on the couch as the kids binge-watched old "Parks and Recreation" episodes and then it happened: my own personal a-ha moment. It struck me when I heard Ron Swanson say, "Never half-ass two things, whole-ass one thing."

Yes. YES. That was it.

This is my whole-ass thing.

Which would be a bitching title, but it seems like publishers wouldn't really go for it even though "Sh** My Dad Says" made it past the literary censors.

Still, my mom would strongly disapprove and would be wildly embarrassed to tell that title to her friends at her church group that makes sandwiches for the homeless.

So, *This.* is it. My Big Gamble. I decided to write a book that I'd want to read, and, full disclosure, I don't really read that much. I did, once upon a time, and I'm pretty sure my voracious, elementary-school reading habits in poor lighting are what led my eyes to their current, dismal state, which is a -11.0 prescription that makes contact lenses a "medical necessity." I really hope what I'm typing makes sense because I can't really read it. The font's so teeny. But back to the kind of book that I like to read…

I either want to be unable to put down that sucker and slam through it in a few days or set it aside when life goes full-throttle tilt but still be able to come back in a week or two and we pick right up where we left off without missing a beat, like best middle-school buddies during the on-again part of our friendship. No re-reading or re-acquainting necessary. I like funny. Nothing sad. Real life is already sad. Why do we need "entertainment" that embarrasses us by making us ugly-cry in public? Ain't nobody got time for that. This is why I will never watch that Richard Gere movie about the dog that keeps going back to the train station to greet his owner even after the guy dies. Some people consider this kind of bittersweet storytelling as life-affirming; well, I say that's why we eat chocolate.

If I've done things right, you will:

A. Feel good about yourself after polishing off a chapter, like you've accomplished something for the day. It's perfectly fine if that chapter was only three pages long. You are a busy, busy person.
B. Have helped me pay for my oldest child's college tuition[*] and, this is the one that really counts, you will…
C. Laugh.

We definitely need to laugh more.

So, here goes nothing…and everything.

Considered (and then rejected) possible book titles:
Mild (as opposed to Wild), Not So Much a Heartbreaking Work of Staggering Genius, The Girl with No Tattoos

---

[*] If you got this from the library, that's great! Those wonderful institutions need to be supported and you shouldn't at all feel bad that my kid will only be able to eat ramen once a day while she's away at college and will likely probably develop rickets because you cheaped out and didn't actually pay for this.

Personal Mission Statement

I believe that…

- brownies are the most perfect dessert and should never, ever be frosted.
- a frosted brownie is just hiding something, most likely inferiority.
- jeans that are truly comfortable and fit well are urban legend.
- Katie never loved Tom.
- getting a free swag bag at any event is the most awesomest thing.
- you can never have too many shoes.
- bacon really does make everything better.
- a bird in the hand is worth…salmonella, most likely, which is why I wear Latex gloves to handle raw chicken.
- children simultaneously make you feel young and suck the life force out of you.
- Fluff is superior to all other marshmallow cremes.
- technology hates me.

A Behind-the-Scenes Look at the Cast and Crew

Halloween 2015, family costume: the Belchers from "Bob's Burgers." Absolutely, positively nobody knew who we were.

Me. Heeeeeey, it's Kristen. We actually just met a few pages ago. Hopefully you remember; if not, I'm screwed.

Joe. aka The Hubster, aka my soulmate, and I'd say Big Daddy but he recently informed me that he hates this and now that I think about it, that term does sound weird in an old-timey way, like a 1950s-ish wife calling her husband that. *Ewww.* Some friends suggested he be named Bert, after the wool "Sesame Street" character hat he wears when he wants to look cool in the winter. So, this guy is my husband of multiple DECADES despite a chronic lack of good judgment, i.e., when he suggested Domino's cater our wedding ("Everyone loves pizza, and they deliver!"). Also, he thinks it's OK to let the kids watch "It's Always Sunny in Philadelphia." No, it's really not. I don't think it's OK for *me* to watch that show.

No. 1. Not gonna lie, she was not my favorite from roughly age 2 to 10. If you could check the browsing history from our computer back then, you'd see a lot of boarding school sites on there. The sass on that kid. As a toddler she yelled at her father, "Don't tell me how to live my life!!!!" His crime: gently suggesting she might not want to wear that pink turtleneck and tights when it was going to be 115 degrees that day. Here's hope for all you parents of teens: She's blossomed into a smart, conscientious, considerate, kindhearted teenager who isn't even vaguely aware of how beautiful she is on the outside — and she's even more beautiful on the inside.

No. 2. Ah, the middle child. This one fits her birth order. Which is crazy since she was the chillest baby ever. Ever.

Barely cried but didn't talk either. In fact, she didn't utter her first word until 2, but now she doesn't ever stop talking and especially not during a movie. You don't want to sit next to her in a theater. Trust me. She deals with many challenges, which are frustrating for her and the rest of our posse. At home we deal with plenty of, uh, let's call it "teen spirit," but every time I visit school, each and every person I come across not only knows her, but praises No. 2 for being the sweetest, most considerate kid. They tell me she's always smiling and excited to be there. So, I'm going to take credit for apparently doing something right.

No. 3. By far the drooliest of my children, he continues to leave a trail of moisture and messiness in his wake. Socks — worn all day and sweaty — are abandoned on the kitchen counter or stuffed between the cushions of my favorite chair. All the Febreze in the world can't erase the stank that blankets the furniture courtesy of his beloved, cotton-blend Nike Elites. As is true of most of his 12-year-old species, he is not ashamed to let rip the foulest farts and loudest burps and laugh hysterically afterward. He also has the sweetest soul. Once, we went to a Triple-A baseball game and the whole ride there, he wore his baseball mitt and talked about how he was going to catch a fly ball. You know what? He DID. He was beyond excited. Then he looked over at the dejected, younger kid standing next to him and without hesitation said, "Here," and handed over the ball.

Dog No. 1. Not my fault. I wasn't even ready for another dog when my husband called me from the Humane Society where he was roaming the aisles. I quickly logged on to its website and tried to steer him past the puppies toward one of the dogs whose write-ups described them as being well-behaved and very…old. (One can only go through housebreaking so many times and I'd just done it with three kids.) He ended up bringing home a black Lab puppy with super-sized feet, which she quickly grew into. We've never ponied up for genetic testing, but based on her personality traits, I'd peg her as a Lab-pig blend. Super bossy, she grabs Dog No. 2 by her collar and drags her around.

Dog No. 2. Again, no genetic testing but personality suggests black Lab-cat mix. IQ testing suggests: potato. And not one of those high-end fancy purple or Yukon gold spuds. We're talking dirt-covered, full of weird sprouty spots garden-variety tater. To wit: The kids tried to play fetch with her and she ran the opposite direction from the tennis ball; she also repeatedly required rescuing when she got her head stuck in the wrought-iron pool fence. Never comes when called and looks for any opportunity to bolt out the front door and go wilding through the neighborhood. She then sits in the front yard and barks indignantly. Worst dog ever. While some members of my family (Joe) will say it's my fault we have her because I happened to wander over to the rescue group and listened to the sob story about how her mother was just adopted and she was all alone, Dog No. 1 is the one who began bonding with her, so I say she's really to blame.

Dog No. 3. Actually No. 2.3 is more accurate because she's little. This one is truly on me. All on me. The kids and I had been volunteering with a rescue group so that they could learn about community service. Pro tip: Parents, unless you want to end up outnumbered by four-legged creatures, don't volunteer with an animal rescue group. This nonprofit saved Australian Shepherds, mostly disabled ones, and helped them find homes. We helped foster one summer and every, single pooch the kids wanted to keep. "No, our job is to help them find a forever home," I told them. Then this sweet, deaf Mini Aussie came along. Her feathery tail wags so hard it careens her body sideways, it even happily thumps in her sleep. I fell for her. Hard. She is a freakishly early riser who conducts her search-and-chewstroy missions at oh-dark-thirty with whatever she finds on the floor (usually Joe's clothes and shoes). She is the biggest turd — and so stinkin' cute and sweet.

Kathy Allen. A dear, dear coworker who is full-on identified by name because she's so kind-hearted, I know she won't sue and I know how much she enjoys taking credit for things and she's really the one who started it all. She made me write a column in the first place. Also, she is the most generous person to ever grace the Earth. This is the kind of person she is: During one particular, on-the-job, blubbery meltdown, induced by being a working mother, she gave me a gift certificate for a massage. It was actually given to her husband, but she stole it from him and gave it to me. And then after another super spaz-out, over the same thing, she gave me her niece. Not in a human trafficking kind of way, of course, but she would pay her great-with-kids-and-never-convicted-of-a-felony niece who would take my challenge child on special outings and give me a much-needed break. That's just beyond.

What You Should Know About the Author

Since we're going to be spending some significant time together with your pants down — let's be honest, it's most likely going to be in the bathroom, which is cool because the same was true of my last gig as a newspaper writer and also, my work often ended up lining bird cages or wrapping breakables and I like that my words were repurposed into something useful — you should know:

- I'm a Taurus, which is dumb to mention because I don't believe or follow that astrological stuff at all. Fun side tangent: I used to work with a woman who would edit out the really mean or bad predictions in the regular horoscope column. Which, while a nice thing to do could also really mess up people when crappy things happened that weren't mentioned in their day's destiny. "My cat's kidneys are failing and she needs expensive treatment? Well that wasn't in my horoscope!"

- I've never really been happy with my hair.
- I've been writing seriously since I was 7. My work before that was pure dreck. While in second grade, instead of playing outside, for a week I plopped down at the dining table after school and wrote about a girl who had a gleamingly beautiful white horse. I got 25 pages into it before I realized I would rather be playing outside with the neighborhood kids.
- I grocery shop at 7 a.m. on Saturdays because I can't handle shopping swarms that kale-block me from the produce.
- I love pranks and jokes and adore April Fools' Day. It's no coincidence that the quasi holiday is my wedding anniversary.
- Over the years, people have said I look like Wonder Woman (the original Lynda Carter version, although I'd be delighted if anyone thought I looked like the 21st century update. To be honest, I think my elbow pits look EXACTLY like hers), Ashley Judd, Lauren Graham and Charlize Theron, but that last observation was made by a waitress (they work for tips) and worse it was said about the time Theron shaved off her eyebrows and got her chubs on to play former prostitute and executed serial killer

Aileen Wuornos in "Monster." I think that was not a compliment. I still tipped, though, because that's the kind of rise-above-it-all person I am.

It strikes me that perhaps I should offer another assessment, like from some independent third party. Here, I'll ask my youngest child because he's too young to drive and pretty much always available.

Me, as I'm taking him out to lunch: "Hey, how would you describe me to one of your friends?"

Him, looking like this could be a trap but could also score him a soda depending on his answer. He starts rubbing his chin as he realizes this is also a comedic opportunity: "Welllllll, she'll brag if she's right. She won't make fun of you, for that long, if you do something stupid — but she will laugh at you. Conversational. Makes friends with strangers."

Huh. I got off pretty easy. And yes, if you were wondering, I did let him order a soda.

Take This Job and…Shelve It, With Apologies to Johnny Paycheck and The Container Store

Nellie Bly. Norma Rae. Karen Silkwood. Erin Brockovich. Elle Woods.

These are some straight-up tough, brave women.

I don't pretend to come even close to their badassery, but I've had my moments.

Like when I was 6 years old and "The Muppet Show" debuted, I fired off a letter to producers, telling them they should, nay, MUST cast me as a Muppet. I didn't want to be a puppeteer, oh no, I wanted to wear a full-on furry costume and appear on my favorite TV show. I told them exactly how tall I was and how much I weighed. Nothing happened. I'll be honest, that still smarts a little even though it's entirely possible that my parents never actually mailed my missive.

Even gutsier, when I was in my early 20s and a supremely untrained, i.e., untalented, singer and actor, I auditioned for a much beloved, local, melodrama theater group. Dressed in a slinky dress with quilted oven mitts hidden behind my back, I sang my very own parody song of "Making Whoopie" called "Making Cookies" because I grew up loving Weird Al* songs and I guarantee it was as painfully goofy as it sounds, although my lovely college roomie who came along for moral support said that I crushed it. Alas, I did not get cast. I am so very thankful this happened during an era when people did not feel compelled to capture everything on cell phones.

So those times, along with the leap-of-faith it takes to become a parent added up to all my bravest moments. That is, until I kinda sorta quit my job. Or, more accurately, I stopped going to it for a while.

Now, truth be told, I'd been thinking about leaving the newspaper for most of the 26 years I spent there. I'd entertain thoughts of something different and occasionally sneak out for job interviews here and there, but ultimately, I

---

* Weird Al was and is my all-time idol, and I would leave my husband for him.

am safe and responsible and not the type to rock the boat. So I stayed. And managed to hang on through multiple layoffs, an increasingly declining industry, reorganizations and revolving through different reporting jobs. What didn't change? That I loved talking with people and then telling their stories…and a regular paycheck. I'd been entrusted with different projects over the years and done well, my stories and columns won awards and while my job satisfaction had never come from a pat on the back from management or a monetary boost, I was starting to realize that there's a fine line between being a dedicated, model employee — and being a chump. I was beginning to feel like the latter.

It's one thing to make allowances for something when you love it. But, I wasn't feeling it any more. The budget got hacked again, reporters worried about another round of layoffs.

The reality was I could make a move now and start over or wait and be involuntarily thrust into the job market in 10 years when I'm older and harder to hire.

"Just quit," urged my husband.

But...but...but...How could I? My Catholic guilt, my overdeveloped sense of responsibility (read Catholic guilt), that need to contribute, the reality of a smart kid who'd likely be attending an ivy-league college all argued against such a drastic move. A small paycheck was better than no paycheck.

"Well, why don't you take a leave of absence?"

Huh. That could work.

And now because the frustrated, still-kinda-dreams-of-being-a-Muppet part of me hopes to one day be vindicated for the local-theater snub decades ago, here's how I envision Lin-Manuel Miranda's adaptation of this book for his Broadway musical "Cook!" He doesn't strike me as the exclamation point type, but I sure am and as creative consultant I will politely but firmly insist on one, if not two.

Cook!!: Act 1

Cook, played by Tina Fey, has already handed her editor a one-sentence note requesting a five-month leave of absence. She and her editor (played by Laura Dern) and coworker Kathy (Sally Field) are whispering about what reaction their main supervisor (Frances McDormand) will have.

Note: Because this is Broadway, it's perfectly acceptable and not unusual to cast age-appropriate actresses. Should this go the Hollywood blockbuster route, then Jennifer Lawrence is me and everyone else cast will be Disney debutante hotties who are less attractive than me, er, JLaw.

SUPERVISOR: KCook, do you want to talk about this note? C'mon, everyone, let's all go into my office so there's not any gossiping later.

Everyone herds into the igloo-ish office, privacy violations be damned.

SUPERVISOR: So, you want to tell me about this letter?

COOK: (clears throat). Well, I've got a lot going on in my life right now, which you'd have read about, if my column hadn't been cut.*

SUPERVISOR (looks impassive).

COOK: (voice shaking a little) Here's the thing — I am a great employee. Management may not realize it, but I do. I

---

* When I did the blow-by-blow account of this meeting originally — which in real life did not involve any explosive devices but did contain the one expletive — at this part of the re-telling No. 1 interrupted to ask, "Wait — did you really say that?!" I assured her I did. "Way to open strong, Mom!"

And that, my friends, is why you stand up for yourself. Because if you don't, then how can you teach your kids to do it? Be brave. All braveness counts, even if it's only a quasi-Johnny Paycheck moment.

have had projects dropped on me, and I've not only done them, I've kicked ass.

COOK smacks over the chair and stands, hands on hips. Editor and coworker Kathy (now played by Lily Tomlin because Kathy changed her mind) flank her, their heads bowed, arms thrust up in the air. A hip-hop infused version of Johnny Paycheck's "Take This Job And Shove It" echoes through the theater.

COOK, *starting to sing*: "Take this job and…shelve it! I ain't working here…for about five months."

Editor and Coworker Kathy dance around the office, circling Cook.

OK, so in the blockbuster version, this would be where I rush out of the office, holding a small grenade in my hand, dramatically pull the pin, toss it in that freakin' cold office and then dive for cover under the metro desk as the charge explodes. Supervisor emerges from her office, coughing, hair all disheveled and black smudges across face. She feebly waves good-bye as I sprint through the newsroom to the door.

"There goes one amazing reporter," she mutters.

Well…That's kind of stupid. But then, so are most blow-'em-up action flicks, which this would most obviously be.

No worries. I'm sure whoever's called in for a re-write will fix it.

End scene.

Momversation: Cashier at the pop-up Halloween shop: "Would you like to round up the bill and donate to charity?"

Me: "What, is that to help impoverished ghouls and boys?"

24 Hours with Me (No Doz Recommended)

A fun feature in a fashion magazine I get for free because of a face cream I bought six months ago features assorted celebs charting for their adoring public a typical 24 hours in their lives. I love reading it because it's just so darn relatable.

The person will talk about waking up at 8:30 — in the morning — and then ringing a bell until someone brings breakfast. The rest of the day is a leisurely blur of probiotic meals prepared by a Food Network chef, personal Pilates sessions and meetings, meetings, meetings! After the personal assistant reminds the VIP that he or she has children, the celeb, of course, lovingly tucks those gorgeous little creatures into bed — and hits the nightclubs.

Pretty amazing lives these people lead.

Well ya know what? I do, too.

A sample of my typical day:

2:30 a.m. Welfare check, performed by my sweet, little deaf dog. She plants her front feet on the edge of my side of the bed to make sure I'm breathing. If I am, I give her a pat. If I fail to immediately respond, she paws at me and sticks her freckled nose in my eye.

3:30 a.m. Another doggie wakeup call. This time, I hear the unmistakable sound of a dog readying to barf. Yup, thar she blows. I roll over — one of the other dogs will eat it.

4 a.m. The third and final dog decides she needs to go out. Now. I stumble out of bed and let her outside.

5 a.m. This is when I usually wake up for good, although I continue to stay in bed buried under the covers as part of the first stage of grief over my loss of sleeping-in-edness. Usually, it's the sound of chewing that snaps me from my slumber. The little dog usually has a slide or maybe a Nerf dart she unearthed from somewhere or a shirt left on the floor. If there's a loud clank before the smacking, then it means she knocked down the toilet seat lid to swipe the TP roll. I'll lay in bed, but the day unspools before my shut eyes — along with the toilet paper — and there's no way I'm sleeping after that.

6 a.m. My husband and I walk the dogs around the neighborhood. The retirees out to enjoy a morning stroll hightail it to the other side of the street upon seeing our two, 90-pound beasts snarling and snapping at the end of

their leashes while the little one alternately helicopters around me in wide circles or lunges forward as if she's a sled dog competing in the Iditarod.

6:30 a.m. The girls are up. "I'm still tired," moans No. 2, as she does every day.

6:40 a.m. Time to shake No. 3 awake, who has managed to remain oblivious to the happy howls of the dogs and the kitchen clanking of his sisters. And who also failed to hear the alarm that he accidentally set for 3:45 a.m. instead of 6:45 a.m. Did I forget to mention that part?

6:50 a.m. "Uh, Mom," No. 3 says, hesitantly, "I just remembered I'm supposed to bring in a dozen hard-boiled eggs."

"When?" I ask, knowing full-well the answer.

He smiles. "Today."

"The only place I know that sells hard-boiled eggs is Trader Joe's and it doesn't open until 8. You'd better Google how to make them."

7:15 a.m. No. 3 starts putting the just-boiled-and-cooled eggs into a baggie to transport to school for a community-service project, making egg-salad sandwiches for a local soup kitchen.

"Dude, you have to peel those first."

He cracks one, plucks off shell attached to a large chunk of white and yolk oozes out.

Ruined. "Those poor homeless people have enough problems, you can't give them food poisoning. Better start calling grocery stores."

Three calls later, boiled eggs are located.

7:30 a.m. Everyone leaves for school and I hop onto the elliptical. I snap on the TV, pedal for 10 minutes and realize No. 3 and I need allergy shots this week, I hop off to make a note in my phone and see that I've already missed three texts from three parents, asking if I can drive their boys to flag football. I thumb out responses.

On the way back to the elliptical, I see the dogs' water bowl is empty. I fill it. Then, I reach down to scoop up the toilet paper pieces scattered across the tile. I go to dump the paper into the laundry-room trash can and it's full. I take it out to the bin and realize it's recycling day. I drag the container down to the curb.

Fifteen minutes have passed, so the elliptical has automatically shut off. It's a sign. I grab a mocha Joe-Joe cookie and shove it into my mouth.

8 a.m. All showered up, I run through emails, check my favorite shopping websites and blogs and settle in to do some writing.

8:30 a.m. I blast out a hilarious tweet.

9 a.m. I remember I was supposed to make cookies for No. 1's volleyball team. No eggs. Damn.

9:30 a.m. Quick run to the grocery store.

12 p.m. No. 2 texts me that she has changed her mind and will no longer hang out in the library after school, so I need to pick her up. The only problem is, school's out at 3:10 p.m. and the flag football crew needs to be picked up from school and driven to the field at 3:05.

1 p.m. My eyes start shutting while I'm sitting upright at the computer, trying to bang out a knee-slapper of a piece on my daily life. Falling asleep while working happens shockingly often.

1:07 p.m. I quit writing for the day and start boiling water for noodles so I can make a quick stirfry that's easily reheated before basketball practice this evening.

3:05 p.m. I load my middle-school charges into the minivan, Uber them out to the field, see that their coach is already there and head back down the road to grab my other kid and drop her off at home.

4:10 p.m. Flag football game is already underway, sunglasses on, it's warm, I'm tired. I may…shut my eyes…for just a little minute.

4:20 p.m. Raucous clapping snaps me from my mini nap.

5 p.m. Game over, it appears we won — yay! No. 3 runs up to me and says, "There aren't enough kids for the B team, so can I stay?" He doesn't wait for an answer and charges back onto the field. Typical. I spy a picnic table with some shade and head to the other side of the field.

6 p.m. Second game ends — one of the teams has won, maybe ours? — and I load up No. 3 and his friend, who also got sucked into staying, and text the friend's mom so she can meet us at our house. He gets picked up. Nuke dinner for No. 3 to eat in the car on the way to basketball practice.

7 p.m. Most of the rest of us eat dinner.

7:30 p.m. No. 1 comes home from volleyball practice, sniffling and dejected. Not a good day. The other adult I live with gets to deal with this while I jet out to grab No. 3.

8:30 p.m. At long last, No. 3 finally cleans up his egg mess from earlier today and then I sit on the couch, iPad propped on my lap…and…Grrrrrriiiiiiiiiiiind, ka chunk, thunk thunk thunk. The very uneasy whir of a not-so-smoothie — second dinner! — being made in the blender wakes me up.

9 p.m. No. 2 sends good-night wishes as she trudges off to bed.

9:20 p.m. Finally time for some TV. My husband who knows how to use the 20 remotes required for watching the living-room television, makes it look effortless as he turns on "Full Frontal with Samantha Bee." I love that show, but it's been a long…yaaaaawwwwn…day…

9:45 p.m. Program's over and I've been asleep since two minutes after it started. Dang it. No. 3 was dispatched to bed in the interim, No. 1 is still hard at work in her room on her homework. Off to bed, until I'm woken up in the wee morning hours by assorted dogs and we do this thing all over again. Hopefully, without the hard-boiled eggs.

My To-Do List: This isn't so much a bucket list as a mini, beach-pail-sized list of things I'd like to do in the near future:

- Learn to play banjo[*]
- Train Dog No. 3 to be therapy dog
- Narrate an episode of "Drunk History"
- Learn to play steel drums
- Take a glass-blowing class

---

[*] If you thought that I was kidding, you're so wrong. Banjo music is great.

That Time I Brought a Newborn to a Fantasy Baseball Draft

What I am about to tell you is absolutely, positively true…I am not embellishing even the slightest. It's all legit.

My first baby was set to arrive Feb. 17, 2000. She ended up being sucked out a day early with some sort of baby Shop-Vac, which I didn't even know was a thing but it is. Aside from a very cone-headed appearance, courtesy of the suckage, she was perfect with this amazing shock of Monchhichi hair (Google them — she really did have as much hair as one of those crazy Japanese monkey dolls from my childhood). I was antsy to get home where I could spend every waking minute memorizing every dimple and detail on her amazing little self except that…I had a fantasy baseball draft to host.

Seriously.

My husband actually scheduled a fantasy baseball draft to be held at our home at the same time that our first baby was due.

I'll tell you something even more outrageous: I am still married to the guy.

Apparently, because he won his fantasy league the previous year, he was obligated to host, regardless of whether the major, life milestone of his first child's birth was happening or not. Guess I'm just thankful I didn't go into labor smack in the middle of the draft. Huh, I wonder which team the baby would have ended up on?

My lovely, considerate mother-in-law drove down from Phoenix for the arrival of her first grandchild — and to handle feeding the crowd of hungry men picking real players for a fake baseball team.

I survived and though I've mostly gotten over it, I figure there is still mileage to be had in that story. Which is why I bring it up. Still.

Flash forward: 17 years later, our youngest child has been bitten by the fantasy bug. Can't get enough. Starts his own fantasy league made up of his school buddies and a few of their dads. I don't pretend to know why this is fun, but usually, it doesn't impact my life, so I tolerate it. Whenever talk at the dinner table turns to names I don't recognize and a sport I don't follow, I just let my eyes glaze over and mentally transport myself to the shoe section of Nordstrom Rack. Now that's my idea of fantasy.

So fantasy football season rolls around — usually the time boots start arriving at the Rack — and talk turns of hosting a draft. Joe, as league commissioner, helpfully volunteers our house.

I know what this means.

"No, no, no, it's easy. I'll handle it," he promised. "You don't have to do anything."

Suuuuuuuure.

Wouldn't you know it, Joe had to make an emergency trip out of town the day before the draft, and was due back…an hour before everyone was supposed to pick players.

Now, I was fully banking on making snacks and vacuuming, but I wasn't prepared when my cell phone blew up, courtesy of some overly pumped papas.

"Hey! Is this an ESPN draft?"

"What time is the draft? Is it eastern time? The app just sent me a reminder, but it said 3 p.m. Eastern…"

"Is it online or offline?"

"Is it limited to 10 people because Josh wants to join…"

"Hey, this is Josh's dad…"

Oh nooooo, I won't have to do a thing.

I experienced probably the fastest ascension in a fantasy sports league ever, promoted from cleaning lady to The Commish in under 15 minutes.

I continued to work the phone lines — texting back and forth with my husband as he worked his way back home from California — while still whipping together Buffalo chicken dip and making the house look presentable enough for a bunch of pre-teen boys and their dads. It didn't take that much effort.

Joe made it home before the first guest arrived (whew) and I was finally off the hook…to do some not-so-fantasy, online shoe shopping.

When you spot multiple plumber's trucks on your street, you're just *bideting* your time until they have to come to your house.

Being the Decision Maker Is Nowhere Near as Fun as Being the Fresh Maker

Here's the scenario: A ski-masked gunman runs up to me and yells, "Your wallet or your life!"

"Uuuuuuuuuuuummmmm…"

It's not that I have a death wish, or a particularly full wallet, I just can't…make…one…more…decision.

I suffer from decision fatigue.

It's a thing, you know, legitimized on the internet with its very own Wikipedia entry and numerous stories on all sorts of reputable journalism sites. And while I have, at times, incorrectly diagnosed myself with Lyme Disease and viral meningitis and a grapefruit-sized ovarian cyst (sadly my poochy belly was just my poochy belly), I know without a doubt I have decision fatigue.

Is there a plastic bracelet or a ribbon for that? Probably not, because I bet no one could settle on a color.

George W may have reveled in being "the decider" but I'm sick of it.

Part of the problem is I'm not just deciding for myself but for four, sometimes five, people in the family and — according to my minivan's owner's manual, I can accommodate up to seven additional passengers — so I am very often also making decisions on behalf of a bunch of bonus kids who need a lift. Take note, future carpooling parents: If you opt for a motorcycle, without sidecar, no one will ever ask if you wouldn't mind also driving little Sophocles to the flag football game, too.

Remember that movie "Minority Report"? Tom Cruise is a futuristic cop solving crimes before they happen and he swipes through all those holographic screens. That's me, in the morning, except I have just one screen and it's a mere 4.7 inches but it holds so, so much information. On a typical day, before 7:30 in the morning, I will have already swiped through all kinds of text messages with assorted people and made dozens of decisions about who's being driven where and when.

Exhausting.

And my husband wonders why he asks a simple question like, "Hey, where should we go on vacation?" and all I can muster is "Uuuuuummmmmmmm…"

I love eating out, but sometimes just looking at a menu, even when there aren't a lot of options, makes my overtaxed brain short circuit. I get all Scarlett O'Hara helpless.

"What do YOU like?" I'll ask the server.

I can't make up my mind even when it comes to something as small potatoes as reading glasses. For months, it's been clear to me — even though printed words have gotten blurrier — that I need reading glasses. I browse the racks at Target, look on websites devoted to cheaters and you know what? I just can't decide. There are so many stinking frames out there. So instead I squint and continue to misdial phone numbers that I just can't make out. Which also makes the carpooling thing all the more complicated.

I could use some help. I haven't had a Magic 8 Ball since middle school, but I'm thinking I might need to get a new one — and with pretty big lettering.

My husband once — and only once — used glitter wrapping paper for my Mother's Day gift and it made him all sparkly like a middle-aged "Twilight" vampire. It was like I got two gifts.

Love Is Like a Box of Chocolates

Gift giving is hard.

Especially for my husband.

Before we were even married, I received — for Christmas and this is not a joke — a cordless phone and set of wooden TV table trays. Even though that didn't bode well, I still went through with the ceremony.

In year six of our marriage, I received the unmistakable pink-striped Victoria's Secret box. Yeah, it was flannel pajamas. And, while I promptly returned them because I took it as an affront to a new mother's sexiness, when 15 years later, this now mother of three was presented with yet another pair of long-sleeved, long-pants flannel jams, this time decorated with doughnuts, those struck me as absolutely perfect.

You'd think — or at least I would — that after two decades and some change, he'd know me. Sometimes he does, like the time I received a FedExed box of Nueske's bacon for my birthday. It accidentally arrived a day early. Still, a box of bacon is the ultimate gift, even if it's a bit of a mixed message. Nothing says "happy birthday" and "hope you don't have many more" than nearly 3 pounds of pig candy. I'm cool with that.

And so, it was with giddy anticipation that I snatched a slim, black-and-white wrapped, rectangular box straight from his hands after he came home from work.

See's!

"Happy Valentine's Day."

"Oooooh! Thank you!" I quickly started unwrapping. "Nuts or chews?"

I'd naturally assumed he'd gone for one of their pre-packaged assortments.

"I picked them out," he said proudly.

Gulp.

This was no box of chocolates — it was a trap. Little relationship landmines all neatly tucked into brown, crinkle-edged cups.

Here was a test, the ultimate test, of our many, many, MANY years together. How well had he studied?

I lifted and gently shook the box. Well, there was his first wrong answer — only one pound?

Inside, neat rows of chocolates lined the box, favorites that I quickly recognized like crunchy molasses chips, a scotchmallow. Woo hoo!

Others, though, were dark circles of mystery. I had no clue. No tell-tale swirls on top to give away what was nestled inside.

I grabbed a knife, readying to perform exploratory surgery on the sweets, see exactly with what I was dealing.

Yellow filling? What?! Nothing chocolate on the outside should ever be that color on the inside.

Maybe the next one would be better. I sliced clean through — blue. Blue? C'mon, See's. You're killing me.

Odd colors aside, he was already failing because I prefer the ooey-gooey caramel-y middles and crunchy, chocolate-covered whole almonds to weird, truffle-ish fruit centers. Ahem, the kind of stuff he, a cheesecake lover (gross), likes.

Just as I was on the verge of contacting a lawyer and drafting a joint-custody agreement for the children, I found redemption.

It was covered in chocolate sprinkles.

A Bordeaux.

I love those. And, and…yes! A mocha!

Awwwwwwwwwww. He does know me!

I took a mental step back and thought about how this wickedly busy guy who's not known for his patience, took a major time-out from his grueling day and drove out of his way to custom-pick a pound of chocolates for his wife. And yeah, some of those bon-bons were more like bomb-bombs, but I also put some blame squarely on See's. Pineapple cream? Really?! That's just so many kinds of wrong and nasty.

This was definitely one case where it's *not* what's on the inside — of the chocolate box, anyway — that really counts.

Truth: I once "enjoyed" Mother's Day dinner at Costco. Could have been worse — I could've had to forage for free samples, but instead a $1.50 drink/Polish sausage combo was generously purchased for me. Another truth: I was not the only mom in the Costco dining area that Sunday. We all exchanged knowing looks that said, "We are buying ourselves some really nice shoes later."

Stomp and Circumstance

Kids need constant protection. It's exhausting. When they're little, it's easy — you just do it for them. You slap spongy corner protectors around the coffee-table edges and stick plastic doohickies over all the electrical outlets. You drop the crib mattress to the lowest setting so they can't climb out. You are in complete control, and they are your sweet, little ~~bitches~~ children.

As they get older, though, you have to switch gears and nurture them by using heart-to-heart talks, which sound like lectures and which don't exactly go over so well with teens because let's face it, parents are lame oldsters who fall asleep on the couch at 9 p.m. on a Friday night and never went to keggers or accidentally left their underwear somewhere other than their butt and were never under 40 so…what the heck do we know?

So, you do what every good parent does: Scare the shit out of them.

In this very specific case, I forced my teenage daughters to take a self-defense class. As frightening as it is to think about turning your innocent kids loose in the big, bad world — without being anywhere nearby to lower their crib mattress and protect them — it's even scarier to divulge to two teenage girls that they are getting out of bed at 6 a.m. on a Saturday. Two weeks in a row.

They were not pleased. Turns out they had plenty of bitter, teen company.

In some sort of mom meme (a momme?), the mothers of No. 1's good friends freaked out at the same time that I did about the possibility of our first-born daughters heading off to college without knowing how to properly drive a dude's nose up through his brain (ya know, if he deserves it). We all ended up sitting near each other at bright and shiny 8 a.m. to learn along with our daughters how to deal with the threats and creepers who lurk everywhere.

Our instructor was none other than Middle-Aged Mr. Clean. A brawny, imposing yet very affable dude, he shared stories — including how an 80-something grandma, the least likely suspect in the house, attacked him with a butter knife — that just go to show, you can't trust anyone ever. You need to be on guard. Always.

Open your own drink at parties. Think it's OK to leave the door to the house unlocked because you have a garage door opener? Think again. Take a selfie if you're on a date with someone you don't know and send it to a friend, just in case. We learned all kinds of stuff, like how to make a proper fist and perform a hammer strike and escape choke holds and wriggle out of a bear hug. We learned enough moves to moonlight as MMA wrestlers. Boy, fights with my brother when I was growing up would have turned out sooooo much differently had I known all this decades ago.

Just when I thought we'd picked up all the defensive maneuvers we could possibly need, we learned more, practicing again and again until we were sore and tired. As I bent over to examine my knee, which was raw from ramming a red pad in the imaginary groin over and over, our instructor told us we could relax.

Um, no, I don't think I'm going to relax ever again.

Part of class — I think this was my favorite — involved yelling. From the diaphragm yelling that would send any wannabe perp running back to his mommy. With every thrust and jab and block, you shout:

"NO! STAND BACK!"

The teens, interestingly, seemed to have a difficult time with this, which is quite contrary to what I've seen in my own home. I, however, have no problem with being loud. No problem at all. At one point No. 1 leaned over to her friends and said, "Yeah, that's how she yells at the dogs."

No matter how many hours are spent learning and practicing how to defend yourself, I don't think it's even possible to feel completely prepared to go into a room and have people attack you, even if it's just pretend. It is disconcerting. Very disconcerting.

I will admit, my body was tense beneath all the assorted protective gear I'd strapped on, yet I still laughed when I caught my first glimpse of an "aggressor." He was suited up in enough padding to look like Ralphie's little brother Randy from "A Christmas Story" — only wearing a helmet and like someone turned a growth ray on him to crank him up over 6 feet tall AND THEN cloned him two times. When I realized I had to get past three, ginormous squishy aggressors, my heart started to pound.

Full of fear and adrenaline and mortifying dread as I realized my panties started riding down at the exact worst time, I faced three, separate attack scenarios that left me breathless and also kind of confused: If my underwear starts falling down does that mean I'm getting chubby or is it just that it's super stretched out and if it's that stretched out, is this from being fat or from being lazy and not hand-washing and air-drying like the care instructions say? Of course I was hoping for the latter. TBD.

"I thought I was going to pee myself," I said, pulling off my helmet when I got back in the classroom.

"You know, probably no one would want to mess with you after that," one of the moms pointed out.

"True," I agreed. "Plus, I'd be pretty slippery."

We all decided that could be a pretty good defensive move, too.

I was feeling fairly triumphant, and maybe just a wee bit like Wonder Woman after what I'd gone through — until they rolled the tape.

Yes, each of us was recorded as we were put through our paces. While I'd felt like I was delivering punishing blows, the actual video of me showed something different. It was reminiscent of cartoon kid fights when one kid starts windmilling his arms frantically and threatening, "Better watch out! If you get in the way and you get hit, it's not my fault." I was not the least bit intimidating. Some minor redemption, though, happened in the final seconds, when I'd managed to topple my attacker and then — I don't know if I was feeling triumphant or just bitchy — but as he lay on the ground, I landed a pretty spectacular parting kick, but in a spot where there were no pads.

"Yeah, that one really hurt," he said, as the scene flashed across the TV.

I felt both badass and just plain bad. Poor guy. Sorry, again.

In the car ride home, the girls and I talked about what we'd experienced.

"It's just really disturbing that we live in a world that's so awful that we have to know how to do this," No. 1 said.

Yes. But, the thing is, you avoid situations that could put you at risk, I explained. You stay alert and smart. The likelihood of having to actually employ what we learned is very, very small.

Hopefully. Please.

"But," I said, "didn't it feel empowering to know how to defend yourself and that you can do it? Didn't it feel good to land some strong blows?"

Because unlike their mother, the video showed that both my girls knew exactly what they were doing.

"Yeah," No. 1 admitted.

"You know what else?" I asked. "When you go back to school Monday and everyone asks how your weekend was, you totally get to say, 'Oh, I kicked some ass.'"

And that is absolutely, positively the truth.

Momversation: My 13-year-old came home from school and informed me he was his school's new pancake eating champion. When I asked what kind of prize you get for such an achievement, he said, "Constipation."

Sh** My Family Says

Justin Halpern — author of "Sh** My Dad Says" — has his infinitely quotable, blunt-speaking father. I have kids.

Who, thankfully, aren't so laissez-faire about dropping f-bombs, but they do say some funny stuff.

Along with the shelves and shelves of photo albums chronicling their every move from birth to around, oh, 7ish, 8ish when I decided they weren't really that cute anymore and I was pretty sick of making super elaborate scrapbooks anyway, is The Notebook. It's just this pink thing with a cupcake on it that I got from the $1 section at Target. Inside is a handwritten rundown of all their bon mots. On occasion, we'll do dramatic recitations from The Notebook, which is at least as entertaining as half of the skits on "Saturday Night Live."

Highly recommend. Not only does it make for a great *momento*, it's infinitely less work than those scrapbooking albums.

Some highlights:

No. 3, age 4, as I reached for his right hand to trim his nails: "That's my sucking hand!"

No. 3, age 4, describing how he'd like his ice cream sundae crafted: "Ice cream and marshmallow and hot fudge with a cherry on the roof."

No. 2, age 7, as she received a squirt of nasal spray: "Fire in the hole!"

No. 1, at the tender age of 8: "I never get a minute to myself. I just want a break!"

No. 2, age 8, the first time she sees Chewbacca in the original "Star Wars": "What's that big guinea pig yelling about?"

No. 3, age 4, after a long day at preschool as he climbs into the car: "Dad, my body's OK, but my head is hot. My hair feels really hot. Could you turn on the hair conditioning?"

No. 3, age 6, to his older sister: "You are the boss of annoying."

No. 3, still 6, on the joys of a new toothbrush: "I'm so happy I got this toothbrush. It feels like a massage for my teeth."

The hubster to our "Hunger Games"-obsessed oldest kid who wanted to take up archery: "If you have to fight for your life in a post-apocalyptic world, you better hope it's a spelling test."

No. 3, age 7, when he pooped and sneezed at the same time: "It was an achoo poo!"

No. 3, on the occasion of his seventh birthday when asked how it felt: "It feels like I'm 6…only older."

No. 2, age 10, while watching an NBA game on TV: "Which team do you want to win? The squeakier one?"

No. 2, age 11, as we pulled into the parking garage of her dad's building: "Is this your hideout?"

No. 2, age 12, reading a cross-stitch in honor of her birth: "A child was born and an angel smiled."

No. 1, age 14: "Are you sure about that?"

No. 3, age 9, offering his review of the wine served at church communion: "The blood of Christ should have some sugar in it."

No. 2, age 12: "If someone married ice cream, then it would be 'lick the bride.'"

No. 1, age 15: "It's OK that they tore down a church to build a Krispy Kreme. It's still a place of worship."

No. 1, age 15, to her sick sibling balking at taking meds: "Natural selection will get you if you don't take your cold medicine."

A sign you're getting older: When you discover the "pillow" lines on your face aren't pillow-related at all.

Enhanced Fitness Technique or Working Out at FiTMO

CrossFit is weird.

I feel qualified to make this judgment because I know about exercise. In fact, I do it. Myself. Every day, even.

I head into the playroom, drop my cellphone onto the weight bench, which is currently being used as a (hopefully) temporary storage area for a carton of electrolyte water bottles and a stack of reusable grocery bags that need to go back in the minivan's trunk, and I hop onto the elliptical for half an hour while I catch up with the Food Network.

Once upon a time, I had a gym membership. The year was 1997 BK (Before Kids).

My husband and I would get up at the butt-crack of dawn, drag our still-sleepy selves down to the gym and squeeze in a workout on machinery sweated on by many others before us. It felt pretty darn good. I even worked out with a trainer for a while. That was another lifetime.

A gym membership these days?

Pbbbblt.

That requires way too much scheduling and planning. Even the possibility of shoe-horning in a visit around busy work and kid-Uber-driving schedules seems too far-fetched. Just not practical. It's much easier to sneak into the playroom for a quickie and — bonus for those, ahem, me, who love multi-tasking — at the same time whittle down the lengthy queue of TV shows gobbling up TiVo's storage.

Although, I s'pose it kind of defeats the purpose when I snap on Food Network, drool over some caloriestrophic concoction like pancake lasagna and then recreate it later that day. For dinner. And that's the end of those 350 calories I burned. Along with about 550 I didn't.

So the other day, I have some time to kill before my hair appointment. I grab a 6-pound carne asada burrito from a nearby drive-through and head to the salon, which is in the same complex as a CrossFit gym. I turn slowly into the parking lot and see the weirdest thing — four people, zombie-shuffling straight down the middle of the parking lot. I squint.

What the?

Thick ropes cinch their waists, and they're dragging metal frames that kind of look like bare-bones sleighs loaded with weights the size of Domino's family XXL-16-inch pizzas. Daaaang.

Wait it gets better — there's a woman dragging a weight-sleigh WITH A BABY STRAPPED TO THE FRONT OF HER BODY. Probably because it would be a violation of gym policy had the baby instead been attached to the sleigh. Hope she got extra credit for that.

I turn off the minivan and adjust the rearview mirror to better watch the CrossFitpocalypse happening on the black asphalt behind me.

Looks hard. I dribble some salsa onto the burrito, which came with French fries tucked inside. Oooh, the salsa's got some serious kick. I feel the burn!

Spicy foods speed up your metabolism, you know. I'm sure I'm incinerating just as many calories as that mom lugging around the baby and the weights — and all I'm doing is eating my lunch.

I spot a guy, comfortably standing in the shade. Trainer perhaps? Huh. Maybe I got some salsa on the mirror and it's sort of impairing my vision but he appears to be dressed…in a naval uniform, Cuban cigar dangling from his mouth. Huh. Appropriate since he is overseeing enhanced fitness techniques, er, training, in Parkinglottanamo Bay.

Hmmm. I guess now that I think about it, I could stand to ratchet up my workouts a bit. I will do that — no more watching Food Network while I exercise. From now on, it'll be low-calorie late-night shows only.

And, even better, I'll start ordering extra-spicy salsa.

Something to consider: What if true strength was measured by the mintiness of the toothpaste a person uses?

Planet of the Apps

Patience is most definitely not one of my virtues.

I have pretty much no patience for anything and especially not grocery shopping. But, it must be done. At least, that's what my needy family tells me whenever the pantry shelves drop to precariously low levels of cereal ("Mom! We only have six boxes left!") and there's only a swallow of milk left in the jug. So, I grocery shop. Grudgingly.

I do plan out meals in advance and make a list, but I haven't the fortitude required for clipping coupons. Shhhh. Don't tell my mom — she would be SO disappointed in me. That woman is such an ace shopper that clerks typically hand her money back by the time everything's bagged. Really.

So screw the coupons, which I brazenly toss into the recycling bin every Sunday without even looking — OK, maybe a quick scan for any Krispy Kreme savings — but now all the supermarkets are getting back at me by adding apps. Click or clip! Well, I've already established I am not in the mood to clip, so I guess I have no choice but to click. Shudder. It annoyed me, but I added some store apps to my phone. Now my email's inbox is cluttered at least twice a week with super special deals "just for U"! I hate that. Spell out the damn word, it's only three letters.

Still, as long as they're trapped in my inbox, I feel compelled to quickly browse the deals since a penny saved is a penny earned toward a new pair of shoes, right? My time is precious, though, and so I am not really sure it's worth it for me to go through all the trouble of clicking and adding my "personalized" coupon for 16-cent habanero peppers because I am pretty sure those things weigh so little that they're free, especially when they "accidentally" get tucked into the cilantro bag. Just kidding, Albertsons. I've never stolen a chile. Ever. Oh look — I "earned" the "personalized price" of $4.74 for Chobani yogurt, which I darn well know only costs $4.99 on sale anyway. Time is money, more than 25 cents' worth, and I don't want to spend a minute logging into the app, finding yogurt from the "eggs and dairy" pull-down menu and then adding it to my list and then clicking it once again to ensure it's in my virtual basket and that true savings will be deducted at the checkout.

Speaking of precious time, when it comes to grocery shopping, I like to get in and out and just be done, which is why I will actually drag myself to the grocery at 7 a.m. on a SATURDAY when only octogenarians dare to shop. But, they're pretty slow, so it's easy for me to whip past them and beat them to the checkout line.

And I realize my annoyance may well be the result of not quite getting this whole 21st century reliance on technology thing because I am a Gen Xer and did not come out of the womb clutching an iPhone. Also, my tech support team (aka, my band of children) is union and it violates the current yearly contract to accompany me on an early-morning food run that falls on a Saturday or Sunday. They sleep in until 11 a.m. Union rules. So, it is entirely possible that I don't have to click around or double-tap as much as I do. There may very well be a shortcut that I just don't know about. Ugh. Apps are such a pain in the ass. Why do grocery stores have to be so diabolical? What's next? Making us scan and bag our own groceries, too? Oh wait…

Momversation: Me, as I watch my messiest kid, shirtless, eat French toast with blueberry sauce: "Good call taking your shirt off."

Him: "I know who I am."

Hi! My Name Is Gary…

I wear many hats: counselor, swagger coach, shopping and shoe consultant, unpaid Uber driver for my kids, unpaid writer, mother, wife, Gary…

Gary?

Yes, I'm a Gary.

If you watch HBO's "Veep," you get it. If not, allow me to momsplain. Gary Walsh is personal assistant to senator/vice president/former president Selina Meyer. He's her "bag man." Not only does he physically tote around anything and everything she needs, he carries a lot of valuable info that he discreetly leans in to whisper on those many occasions she's caught completely blank. In one episode a few years back, the two get into a fight and Selina dismisses him as unimportant, but Gary fights back with all he does for her: "I'm your calendar. I'm your Google. I'm your Wilson the volleyball."

Yup. That's me.

I've been married for a looooong time and I'm a pretty good wife, but I'm a really good Gary. I bail my husband out on a regular basis. He's a top-tier guy and all but he's, well, bad with names and faces and overall general remembering. Yes, I think that pretty much sums it up. I'll share some recent examples:

Scenario 1, at a charity event with a lot of faces swirling around.

Him: "That guy, over there. Do we know him from somewhere?"

Me: "Yes, he used to be your boss."

Him: "Ooooh yeah."

Scenario 2, shopping at Costco.

Him: "That lady, she's walking toward us, like she knows us but she's scowling. Who is that?"

Me: "That's my parole officer."

Scenario 3, in the living room.

Him: "That kid, over there, she looks really familiar..."

Me: "That's our oldest child, born Feb. 16, 2000. She's been really busy with school and scholarship applications and has been holed up in her room, so you haven't seen much of her."

Just kidding about that last one. Oh, and, ahem, the one before that. OK, and even the first one, too. I exaggerate, but I really do have to ID people for him everywhere we go.

I helpfully text reminders about birthdays for family and friends and even his coworkers and usually add "Gary" at the end of them. But I tell you, I am paying the price. My brain is so bogged down with important (and not-so-important) dates and information that it's the mental equivalent of me schlepping all his stuff around for him. It's exhausting. I like to think that it's because my gray matter is so crowded with day-to-day hoo-ha that this is why my kids think I'm stupid for being unable to remember basic facts I learned in school, like what is the capital of Wisconsin? Or, where is the Gobi Desert?

Do you know what I learned the other day? That narwhals are REAL. They're real, people! I always just assumed they were fake, some sort of unicorns of the sea. When I shared my newfound factoid at dinner, the kids were dumbfounded.

"Wow, Mom…" No. 1 said, rolling her eyes.

So, I guess I'm not foolproof, but you know what? I come through when it matters — like when my husband couldn't remember where he'd left his work bag or his badge. I knew exactly where to find 'em. Now, if I could only remember where MY keys are…

I earned my middle-school-aged son's respect by admitting to him — on a cold day in February in Portland, Ore. — that I needed to fart but didn't want to lose any body heat.

There's No Crying[*] in Parenting

We have plenty of smiley photos in our albums. Lots. These do not tell the real story.

---

[*] Actually, there is. A lot of it.

One photo does. You're looking at it. This one totally tells it like it is. No. 1, age 5, valiantly tries to keep squirmy 1-year-old No. 3 on her lap. Her mouth is open, as she tries to sooth his annoyance. His shirt has ridden up to expose the kind of belly you only see painted at Chicago Bears games. No. 2, ever the troublemaker, is full-on crying. She wants snack.

This is not an Anne Geddes moment. Not by a long shot. But I sure wanted it to be, so I had everything set up for the perfect picture that would highlight three, not-so-perfect but very cute, cherubic children. I can laugh at this picture now. This one, it truly is worth a thousand words — a thousand words on why you should think really, *really* hard about becoming a parent because it is not easy. It is exhausting and the kids won't cooperate and anything that can go wrong, will and you just have to roll with it. Even better if you laugh. I was not laughing on this day.

At the exact moment this shot was snapped, I almost snapped. Actually, I'm pretty sure I did.

These child models being the testy, petulant creatures they are, would not cooperate. Well, one did. I'll admit it: She's my favorite. She tried to rally the troops, but alas, the perfect photo was not to be.

I believe my tirade went something along the lines of "ALL I WANT IS ONE LOUSY PICTURE! IS THAT SO

MUCH TO ASK? I'M YOUR MOTHER! C'MON! GIVE
ME A BREAK! JUST ONE LITTLE BREAK! I'LL GIVE
YOU GOLDFISH! YOU CAN WATCH TV! JUST,
PLEASE, FOR TWO SECONDS, CAN YOU
COOPERATE?! IS THAT SO HARD?! I DO SOOOOO
MUCH FOR YOU! YOU CAN'T DO THIS ONE, TEENY
THING FOR ME?! YOU ARE GOING TO BE SO SAD AT
CHRISTMAS!"

It makes me laugh when I see the perfect, posed family
pictures on Facebook — because I know the truth. It's the
outtakes that tell the real story. Families are messy, tough.
It's not easy, it just…is.

So you take the good, you take the bad, you take them
both and there you have…the facts of life. Who would have
thought the theme song from an '80s TV show could be so
spot-on? But it is.

Every time I drive No. 1's car, I'm always taken aback
by all the used Kleenex tucked everywhere. I prefer to
believe that she's crafty and handmaking her own airbags
and that she's not really just a slob with allergies.

Get Your Slop Here!

This time, I am not missing out. No way.

In the '80s, I was late to the leg warmer party. Then, I was oblivious to the whole placenta-eating trend with all three of my kids. But I am bound and determined not to miss out on the current craze sweeping the nation — the lifestyle brand.

After several long seconds of deep, contemplative thought and soul searching, I'm switching gears to launch Slop (pat pending).

My inspiration: none other than Ms. Gwyneth Paltrow. She was talking about her side hustle (not to be confused with side boob, although I guess for some celebrities they could be one and the same) on "The Late Show with Stephen Colbert" when I had my very own ah-yoni moment and realized…Oh snap! I could make A LOT of money.

These are desperate, troubled times and yet a lot of people out there still have plenty of disposable income to go along with the nagging emptiness that compels them to engage in conspicuous consumption of material goods in the pursuit of owning something, anything, that's expensive enough to plug that hole in your heart and reduce the angst that haunts the very sole. Yes, sole. New shoes will take care of that! What also helps? Ponying up for one or more of these new, highly exclusive offerings from Slop. Yes, folks, it's true: You can restore hope and regain your faith and get firmer thighs, too, all it takes is your credit card:

• **Personal Chakra Shack Center.** We all need a place to escape, but if you don't have a safe house or a second home in the Hamptons, this is the next bestest thing. Use all the muscle you have to pry the sticky, plastic door open and once inside, after you push away the shovels and extra ceramic tile and the still-inflated dolphin pool toy, you can get down to meditative business. Shut out the distractions of modern day life and give your weary mind a break while awakening your senses to the extreme cold or

heat and maybe get the slightest buzz off the gas fumes emanating from the leaky leaf blower. $198 per quarter-hour of meditation.

• **Bite Me Vitacalifragilisticsexpiali Dose Us Vitamins** With Ginseng and Turmeric and Added Calcium. These chewy, holistic supplements are designed to be calming while energizing and they're chockfull of wellness and

maybe just a smidge of meth. They'll boost your metabolism, make your immune system invincible, crank up your level of alertness, help your vision, sharpen your hearing and then bring on the ultimate release as you come crashing into a state of utter and complete coma, er, calmness. They're tart, they're sweet, they're a good workout for slack jaws. They're blended with a special herb grown high in the Andes and harvested by only the most virtuous of the pack of regional wild guanacos that pre-chew the herb for maximum flavor and absorption. Also, they may contain the tears shed by Gwyneth Paltrow who's now scared of her newest competition. These have no actual medicinal effect but may make you feel smug. Also, also, these are not repackaged Sour Patch Kids. $500 per 10-tablet pack. Dosage: 10 tablets approximately every 10 minutes.

- **Recycled Organic Hydration Cloak.** Everyone knows

how important hydration is, but not everyone needs to know you carry an off-brand water bottle. Keep that cheap thing under cover with one of these thick, artisanal pieces in a variety of patterns and colors. They're not my kids' unmatched socks. Swearsies. $299 each. Please allow us to personally select a cloak for you.

• **Petromorphic De-Stressing Meditators.** Oh please, they're not rocks! These rough-hewn mini boulders are carefully handcrafted by Mother Nature — and the strong teeth of Labs that enjoy chewing nonfood items. Directions for use: Gently roll them around in your palms because they're kind of sharp, and then feel a stab of calm. If you feel an actual stab because you punctured your hand and are bleeding profusely, well,  then you're guaranteed to reach an ultra high level of calm that could cause you to pass out. Another suggested use: Hurl directly at the person who's crushing your chill. $599.99 per dozen.

• **Manual Labor.** Sometimes our lives feel just so devoid of purpose. Our jobs are mind numbing and pointless. What's it all about? This lets you get back to basics when life was simpler and allows you to feel and really see that you have accomplished something with your valuable time. It feels great to get down and dirty and so you should definitely

come clean out my minivan. Guaranteed good for the chakras. Also, guaranteed weight-loss — if you use your own spit to clean the windshield. $1,999.99.

I think a really cool expression would be "I like the cut of your *glib*." Let's see if we can get that going.

Today's Youth Don't Know How to Barf

What is wrong with kids today?

I'm not referring to how they're losing their ability to make eye contact or that they're scared to use phones for actual talking. No, the 20th century skill that seems to be fading away into obscurity in the 21st century is the ability to know how to hurl, call Ralph on the porcelain telephone. Oh wait, maybe I should use another euphemism more easily understood in these times, like downloading dinner. I'm talking about, if you didn't guess already, throwing up.

I always assumed this was one of those natural instincts. Apparently not.

Do kids just not know what to do because they aren't barfing as much as in the olden days when I threw, er, grew up? Is all that antibacterial soap on the market making for less gastrointestinal upset? Like how chicken pox — that scourge of my Gen X youth that subjected me and my peers to crackly coatings of pink calamine lotion like some sort of introductory step to a Pinterest project for crafting a human piñata — has been largely but not fully eradicated? I say not fully because when I discovered No. 3 had pink, multiplying bumps on his torso in second grade, I assumed it was bed bugs and threw out his mattress and then when I booked an appointment with his pediatrician, she had to call in another doc for a second opinion to confirm that yup, even though he was vaccinated, he was one of those lucky ones to acquire chicken pox anyway.

In my own house, my kids rarely complained when they were little that they needed to ralph. Once, and only once, did my oldest child say that her stomach felt really, really weird. I explained that if she needed to throw up, she better run right to the toilet. She followed orders: She charged into the bathroom, sat down on the commode and promptly threw up all over the floor.

So perhaps puking — like math skills — skips a generation? When I was a kid, regurgitating was my jam, my go-to move no matter where I was. At the risk of sounding like a Dr. Seuss book specifically written for pediatricians' offices, I yakked at school, at birthday parties, in the car, on planes, here, there, everywhere.

I knew exactly what to do, too — kneel, pull back my hair and stick my head in the toilet. I didn't outgrow my vomitus behavior either. As old as 15 — yes, way old enough to know better — on a California road trip, my family ducked into a restaurant we'd seen advertised on billboard after billboard — Pea Soup Andersen's, known for its thick, hearty bottomless bowls. Well, you can guess where this is leading.

Andersen's serves 2 million plus bowls of pea soup a year, and I had just finished my own personal second when someone made me laugh so hard that I gagged and…You know what happened. At least I had an empty bowl in front of me. I refilled it, much to the confusion of our waiter who'd checked on the table moments before, noted the ready-to-be-cleared dish and was coming back to retrieve it.

Decades later, I still worship the porcelain goddess. Things got really bad when I was pregnant. We'd go out to eat and I would immediately throw up in the parking lot or, once, in the bushes of our friends' front yard after they'd served us a home-cooked meal. My husband said he was going to start asking waiters if we could rent, rather than straight-out buy, my meals.

So, where am I going with this? Not sure, but it seems worth mentioning. When I queried parents on Facebook if their kids knew how to, shall we say, bring up the vote, so many did not. I think it's time to start a grassroots effort to make this part of the core curriculum. So maybe along with reading, writing and 'rithmetic we need to add ralphing —

as in, how to — to the kindergarten mix. Who's with me? Pretty sure the school janitors will be on my side.

Momversation: Kid No. 1, examining an old-ish yogurt container: "Can I still eat this if it says expires June 30."

Me: "Of course, yogurt already tastes expired."

Quick! Call Flo or the Lizard! The Joys of Adding a Teenager to Your Car Insurance Policy

I'm a lifetime past 16, but I still remember driving lessons.

My dad was usually the one who took me out onto the road. We started in a church parking lot and then I worked my way up to a lightly traveled stretch of asphalt out in the county.

Body rigid, hands at 2 and 10, eyes darting from the road to the rearview mirror, my muscles ached from the tension.

My dad always played it cool and was fairly subtle when doing the fake brake with his right foot when I was going too fast and he kept his fingers perpetually hooked over the bar above the window, so it wasn't completely obvious when he was bracing himself for impact.

"Look out for the cow," he said casually.

Sure enough, there was a black and white one by the side of the road.

I glanced that way and the 1971 Ford Galaxy 500 under my complete power started drifting in that direction.

My dad lost it.

"I said look out for it! Don't hit it! Geez!"

Luckily, I was well under the speed limit — for 1940. That cow had plenty of time to get out of the way.

Flash forward 30 years, and I'm taking my own daughter out to cruise.

Because it was tradition — and seemed like good juju — we also held our very first lessons in a nearby church parking lot. Despite my best attempts at playing it cool, 12 mph had never felt so fast and I found myself sucking in my breath and bracing myself. No. 1 noticed.

We survived those lessons, our relationship mostly intact, and after she scored her license, I thought the hard part was over — then we had to add her to our insurance.

Woof.

Double woof because, our amazing, talented oldest child — who gets a good student discount and also completed a five-hour safe-driving program, offered by our local police department on the same course that first responders are trained — had two accidents within a month of getting a license. The first victim was the right post holding up our carport and the second, a parked car at the mall that she tapped as she pulled out of a spot.

Whoops.

Not to be outdone by a new, whippersnapper driver, my husband then felt compelled to get both speeding and parking tickets on our summer vacation. I would have preferred a less expensive souvenir, perhaps a T-shirt that said "Seattle."

So when that insurance bill arrived, I could hear the scream on the other side of the house.

"Oh my God! Our car insurance for six months is $1,600! Guess it's time to look around."

Insurance Call No. 1: He clicks on the speaker — presumably so I can enjoy from the living room — and dials. Soon I hear a chirpy guy introducing himself and asking whom he's speaking with.

"OK, Joe," says the happiest sounding person ever to sell insurance, "so the first thing I need you to do is to pick a special password that only you know, that you can use when you call us on the phone so we know it's you, Joe."

Wait, did he call an insurance company or some kinky hotline?

Then, just to drive the point home, Chirpy McChirperson said again, "Only you can know this word. It could also be a phrase — a word or a phrase, but no one else can know it, not even your wife."

This is the point I wanted to yell from the other room that he was on speaker phone, but I also wanted to see where this was going. Plus, I wanted to hear what this super-duper, exempt from spousal privilege word was gonna be.

Joe hemmed and hawed for a few minutes, but landed on his very own super special, for-this-insurance-company-only word or phrase. And, I still remember it. Bwahahahahahahaha! Sorry, Chirpy.

The conversation went on for a good 20 minutes about different, but all boring, aspects of coverage for cars, for the house. Blah, blah, blah. I listened to every word.

End result: That auto insurance was $2,400. So much for a better rate.

For all their "no one can know your special word or phrase" talk, they certainly were not shy about copying me, via email, about all the different insurance scenarios Joe talked over with the Chirpster. I received no less than 20

emails after their conversation ended. Wait a minute...
were they trying to alert me? Was he looking into a life
insurance policy FOR ME? Oh snap. I'd better go dig those
out of the e-trash.

Truth: When you grow up in the desert, real winter
weather can throw you for a loop. To wit: No. 1 was freshly
driver's-licensed and hadn't been on the roads for very long
when a severe cold snap hit. It was early in the morning
when she headed out the door for school and soon was
back in the house. "Something's wrong with the
windshield! I can't see out of it!"

That, we explained, is ice. Then we showed her how to
use the defrost setting on the car. Once she arrived at
school, all her friends reported having the same problem
and no one knew what to do, especially not the girl who
actually hung her head out the window so she could see.

That Time Bobby Flay Tried to Poison Me

OK, so maybe on second thought, this chapter title strikes as a little too inflammatory. Still, it is true.

Mostly true.

Even if it wasn't intentional.

It's not like the wildly popular Food Network celeb chef poured strychnine straight onto my plate, but he might as well have — he slid eggs onto it.

Which very nearly made me throw up on a nationally televised, cable television show, which continued to run years after its original airing, causing random parents from school to look at me slightly askance like they recognized me from somewhere but weren't sure where.

Or, maybe I just had food on my face.

Probably the ep still pops up early, early mornings before paid programming featuring the veggie spiralizer doohickie, which I've gotta say, is tempting me.

But, I'm getting ahead of myself.

Let's back up.

Sometimes, unexpected things happen. Like the phone rings and it's the Food Network and they need a local food writer familiar with regional cuisine for some mystery show.

My camera-shy coworker Kathy Allen, who actually fielded the call, took a hard pass.

"Hang on, I'm going to send you over to Kristen Cook. She'd be perfect."

Wait? What?

And that was how I ended up on a Food Network TV show — without the benefit of a hair and makeup person.

Apparently, the network prefers to spend all its money on ingredients and sending its stars to exotic locales like Tucson, Ariz.

For weeks, I'd chat occasionally with a producer who'd ask me to pretend I was giving a food review or how I'd describe certain foods. I'd try and squeeze in a question about the unnamed TV show, but it was like trying to pry information out of a very well-trained spy — or my own children.

Me: "So this show that might tape here, is it 'Throwdown with Bobby Flay' because it kind of sounds…"

Her: "OK, getting back to breakfast dishes…"

The producer later revealed that I was thisclose to getting kicked off the show before it even taped because of my extreme nosiness. Those Food Network folks are a secretive bunch. The whole experience was so cloak-and-dagger that I had to sign about 20 pages of documents in which I legally pinky-swore not to disclose anything before airing, lest I be sued for a million dollars. Ha! The joke would have been on them! Good luck trying to wring a million dollars out of a reporter working for a paper in a mid-sized market!

Just at the point when I had pretty much forgotten the whole thing, I got a phone call telling me to report to a particular downtown hotel precisely at 10 a.m.

Turns out my suspicions were spot-on as I glanced out a window and spied Flay, in all his red-headed glory, sauntering down the sidewalk, flanked by TV cameras. This was indeed an episode of "Throwdown," which pits mere mortal, local chefs against the suave, flame-haired celeb in a culinary competition to see whose version of a specialty is better.

The other judge, a well-respected chef from Phoenix, was pure badass. She had close-cropped hair, tinted glasses, tattoos and roared up in a black sports car.

And there I sat, in my gray twinset, looking like a marriage counselor who has a higher divorce rate that she'd care to admit.

At one point, the producers made us stand back to back, arms folded, serious expressions knitted on our faces for what was called "the hero shot." (Side note: I don't think I've ever heard my children cackle harder than when that very image appeared on screen.)

But, what scared me — even more than the fact that I was responsible for my own primping — was what I might be eating on this show. Turned out I was right to be afraid, very afraid: The featured regional breakfast food was none other than huevos rancheros. Eggs. Rancher's eggs.

Ooooohh FFFFFFFFF...Fieri! Guy Fieri would feel my pain. He hates the little yolkers, too.

Full dishclosure: The one thing Fieri and I have in common is that we were both attacked by chickens as children. OK, well, I don't exactly know why Fieri hates eggs — I already told you those Food Network peeps are so tightlipped — but I was routinely tormented by my grandparents' evil red rooster, who didn't lay eggs himself but he consorted with the chickens that did. Also, eggs taste nasty. They're gross. I hate them unless they are appropriately and safely hidden away inside cake or cookies.

Just the smell of liquid chickens cooking triggers my gag reflex. I knew I was going to hurl. All over Bobby Flay.

And, he already thought I was an idiot because when I was supposed to enter the room and specifically shake hands with all the competitors, I ignored him. Blew right by him, requiring another take.

"Hey, you didn't walk past me this time," he said on the second run-through.

Mortifying.

Then, it was time to judge. Gulp.

Dish A smacked of Flayness: crisply fried tortillas topped with a fluffy white disc with a fat yellow dome in the middle, which looked very much like a zit waiting to pop, along with spicy crumbles of chorizo and a drizzle of deep burgundy chile sauce.

Dish B was a massive mound of beans, green Hatch chiles and warm blankets of melted cheese. No eggs to be seen, but they were in there. Hiding. Waiting to make me gag.

While my fellow judge complained about the too-thin sauce and runny beans, I took a bite and tasted egg. Only egg.

It took all my willpower not to barf.

We leaned in to whisper, building suspense as the producers had urged us to do before the taping.

"I liked 'A' better," my partner said. I agreed. "'A' is definitely Bobby Flay's."

"Then should we pick 'B'?" she asked.

"No, I think we should be honest," I told her. I'm such a Girl Scout, as evidenced by my matchy-matchy twinset outfit.

And that is how Bobby Flay won the Season 8, Episode 6 huevos rancheros "Throwdown," much to his chagrin, at least according to his assistant who told us afterward that he hates to beat the local chefs.

That would have been good to know before I ended up with a brief stint as Tucson's most hated resident when the restaurant owners and numerous readers called and emailed to complain about the story I wrote describing my brief fling as a Food Network personality. They all felt it besmirched not only a beloved regional breakfast food but also a very popular local Mexican restaurant. There is a surprising number of egg lovers out there.

Whatever. At least I didn't throw up on Bobby Flay.

Truth: I like to keep an expired can of Wu Chung White Fungus ("Ready to Serve!") in the pantry as a gentle reminder to my kids that yes, actually, I could serve you something way worse than roasted beets.

Men Are from Mars, Women Don't Like Shopping for Recliners

If I had to nail down our interior decorating style, I'd describe it as…frat house on probation. Sigma Crappa chic.

It's really not a genre you see depicted on the Home & Garden channel or anywhere really, except, of course, said frat house and maybe the occasional crack den.

If you're having trouble pinning down what exactly constitutes this particular design style, allow me to paint a picture. Imagine mismatched furniture — on-sale floor models, mostly, along with a cream leather recliner, something that would look perfect on the bridge of the starship Enterprise. It was gifted to us from the in-laws, as is the case with key pieces of furniture in our family and play rooms.

Continuing with the tour, fuzzy blankets, all with holes chewed into them by a current four-legged resident, are wadded up and left strewn across all available seating space. A $15, long-legged end table from Target is turned on its side and angled across the olive-hued chair and a half. It's supposed to deter the nastiest of all the dogs — the one that goes in and out of the pool and then roots around in the dirt for critters to maim and bring in the house and she spends 90 percent of her time obsessively licking the fur off her butt — from etching her stank into the microsuede fabric. The chair's giant matching ottoman has a spot chomped out of it, all the way through to the wood thanks to a previous four-legged resident. The nice thing is, another spot just like it exists on the edge diagonally across so that no matter which way you turn the ottoman, your guests can see that only the finest plywood crafted from recycled No. 2 pencils was used to create such a magnificent and obviously tasty, if not tasteful, piece.

This is my living room.

It's nasty. I have accepted it.

My husband — who once was fine with the hot mess — has had his eyes opened. All it took was one innocent peek into a Pottery Barn store. Now he's obsessed with becoming the host of his very own HGTV makeover show. I hate those programs.

He's accumulated all these leather swatches with names like Brompton and Berkshire, which you damn well know were on the shortlist for Gywneth Paltrow's children. He's got some new friends — Ileana and Frank, pronounced Fraaaaaaahnk — who are in-house interior decorators for swank furniture stores and leave messages on our home phone about their thoughts on configurations and the merits of having a coffee table versus not.

On an almost daily basis, he'll look over the living room and mutter, "Oh my God."

This is impressive because he has a pretty high tolerance level for filth. Once, as part of an experiment — yeah, it was a sciiiiieence experiment and not at all laziness — I skipped washing dishes to see how many days it would take before he tackled them. "The last time I saw a kitchen like this, it was on 'Cops,'" he groused. Then he scrubbed and dried for an hour. Length of time that had passed: a week. It took him exactly 13 years to gather up that similar level of disgust for the living room.

Because he is a guy, he first zeroed in on recliners. According to my friend who's an interior designer, all men love recliners and all women hate them. I know I do. To me, they scream "I've had a long day and now I need to undo the top button on my pants and crack open a brewski." Not a fan. Although I will admit to enjoying undoing the top bottom on my jeans as soon as I get home.

"Ooooh. Look at these," the husband offered, showing me a high-end website that offered not just one recliner but an entire connected row of them.

Trading frat house for movie house is not my idea of an upgrade. Actually, it's not that far of a leap from our current situation — we already have sticky floors and an absurd amount of popcorn scattered around.

For months, he's been scouring websites and dragging me into furniture stores to look at stuff. At least I can sit.

On vacation in California, we split up on a shopping trip because he didn't want to go into Lululemon ("They have guy stuff!" I told him) and then he texted that he was in Restoration Hardware. For the uninitiated (that would be moi), this is no ordinary furniture store. It is the Shangri-La of furniture stores.

The kids and I wandered down the street, peering into storefronts trying to find him. We came upon what looked like an incredibly fancy hotel. The entire front was completely open air, with sumptuous couches and chairs set up in classy, aesthetically pleasing vignettes. I could have sworn I saw a circular concierge desk in the middle of it all. It looked very much like a resort, one with a lot of furniture.

"What is this? Is this place a hotel?" I asked, confused. "This can't be Restoration Hardware."

"Well, here's a sign that says 'RH,' so I think this is it," No. 1 said.

Even the elevator — with its long, black leather-cushioned bench and ornate gold mirror — was nicer than any room in my house.

And yet, despite the luxury, it seemed so homey, comfortable enough for No. 2 to crawl completely under the covers of a luxurious king-size bed and for a guy to break things off with a girlfriend as they were seated across from each other at a reclaimed Russian oak rectangular parsons dining table. That is absolutely true — as far as we could eavesdrop. A dude actually ended a relationship right there in the Restoration Hardware on Melrose.

"You're a nice person, I just don't see you in my life..."

"Wow, I'm glad we don't have that salesman," No. 3 muttered after we'd quickly walked past.

His dad explained to him that he had just partially witnessed a breakup and not a furniture deal falling through. Harsh.

But, really I guess the guy did that woman a favor because in the long run, it will be so much more economical that her emotional scars will never allow her to set foot in that store again.

While our family breadwinner talked with a salesman about seat cushion depth and the merits of a 9-foot couch (which sounds very much like a song title that Southern Culture on the Skids would come up with), the rest of us draped ourselves across the leather Maxwell sofa, scooching our cheeks into those cushions to leave butt grooves that the cleaning crew would have to fluff out later. The menfolk talked about the multiple layers of wax lovingly applied to the hides and then polished to bring out highlights and lowlights that develop with age. I dragged my nails across the cushion — pretending I was in a middle-school girl fight — in an effort to simulate the *petina* that would no doubt develop in our three-dog household.

So, get this: Now we're in Phase 2. In an exciting twist, things are all jumbled up in a new arrangement on a daily basis to simulate what the living room would look like with a sectional or maybe even a long couch with a chaise.

The husband still trolls furniture sites, and the occasional crack of a tape measure snapping back into its metal case will remind me that no, this isn't over. Not yet.

A new dog bed was even brought into the house in an effort to train the four-legged family members that this is where they really belong. I dunno if that's gonna work.

Maybe if we upholstered that bed in top-grain, pure aniline Berkshire leather with a warm, matte chestnut finish. Then we could all pile on that and show them how it feels.

"Take that, dogs! Now we're on your furniture!"

In fact, No. 3 does actually occasionally crawl onto the new dog bed. He says it's comfortable.

Mental note: We should get him checked out.

Basically, we all know who the real winners are here in this situation. They have four legs, and they've already scored a new bed. It's quite likely they'll end up with a whole new set of furniture, too.

Truth: While watching "Memento" for a second time, my husband notes, without the least bit of irony, "I forget what happens in this movie…"

And Puppy Makes Three

I had it made.

I was totally, completely in the clear. Sleeping in was mine. And I blew it. Blew. It.

Like most parents, I have lost the equivalent of oh, I'd say a decade, of sleep. Feedings, poopings, peeings, monster-sightings, Christmas Eve excitement, meltdowns, they have all taken their toll. And, just so you know, if I had my way, I'd get nine hours of sleep a night. That hasn't happened since I was 29, unless you count that one time in 2009 when I was super sick with some self-diagnosed flu-meningitis hybrid, and actually, come to think of it I was probably actually in a coma.

If you count that, and I do, that was my last good rest.

But I'm at that point in parenthood, that glorious and yet highly annoying time when my kids would all willingly snooze for a month solid. It's an amazing tectonic shift in sleep patterns and yet I'm still up at 5 a.m., or more often, 4 a.m., because I brought the ultimate morning person into our house: a little dog.

It's on me. My bad.

In an effort to teach the kids about the importance of volunteerism, I joined up with a rescue group dedicated to helping special-needs dogs.

Even Daredevil can see where this is going.

We manned information booths at events and would help care for foster dogs that stayed at someone else's house. It was a pretty good deal — play and feed the dogs without the wear and tear on your own house and heart.

Initially, each new dog that came along, the kids would beg to keep.

"Pppppllllleeease!"

Nope, I told them, we're helping these dogs find their forever homes. We can't keep them. Plus, we have two, almost pony-sized dogs at home. Our house can barely contain all of the two- and four-legged creatures in it.

Then she came along.

Snowy white with a freckled pink-and-brown nose and pale-blue eyes that sometimes seemed to go in opposite directions, she was all ears and tail. Charmingly, that tail even wagged when she slept.

None of the kids asked to bring her home. Instead, I was the one who sheepishly told my husband I'd fallen in love.

"I know I said no other dogs or pets, but…"

She was so small, not even 20 pounds, and super chill. She did happen to be deaf, but that wouldn't be a deal-breaker. In fact, she'd be right at home. No one else in the house listens to me either.

The process of adopting this little deaf dog was intense. I'm fairly sure convicted murderers, still in jail, trying to adopt a kid would have an easier time. I was ready to give up when we finally got the OK that she was ours.

Well, mostly mine.

She loves one and all, but I'm the only person lucky enough to get early-morning welfare checks. She slaps her front paws onto the edge of the bed frame and sticks her face close to mine to make sure I'm still there. I am.

I'm the one who groggily stumbles out of bed to rescue Kleenex and toilet paper from her manic, morning attacks, which typically start around 4 a.m. She loves her morning walk with the big dogs and Tigger-bounces into her crate when it's time for breakfast. Then, by 9 a.m., she's wiped out. Exhausted. She curls into a tight ball like an arctic fox, tucking her nose under her paw, and that's how she'll stay, on the couch, until I poke her awake. Which I most certainly feel entitled to do.

"Hey!" I shout, even if she can't hear.

If I don't get to sleep, why should she? Fair is fair.

She's a constant thorn in the side of Dumb Dog No. 1 and Dumb Dog No. 2 because she loves being around them, too, following behind them like an annoying younger sibling as they race after lizards. She plops down next to them, any time they're lying on the floor, wriggling close enough to have her butt and tail right in their noses. If those two could ask for some cool evolutionary assist to help in their destructo-dog ways, it wouldn't be opposable thumbs to better get at the garbage and the food on the counter. Noooooooooo. They'd ask for middle fingers so they could thank us properly for bringing her home.

Lucky people find money in their pockets. I usually discover Kleenex. Used.

It's OK to Hold a Grudge if It Saves Calories

First let me acknowledge that I know there's something wrong with me.

I shouldn't hold grudges like I'm Inigo Montoya avenging his father's death. But at the same time, I think there should be consequences for removing my favorite salad from the menu.

No, restaurants, you don't want to make me angry because I hold a grubge. That would be grub plus grudge and specifically applies to grievances I have against assorted eating establishments around town. We'll pass by one such restaurant and a kid will point out, "We can't eat there anymore. Mom's mad at them."

One chain restaurant I won't go to any more because I got my very first case of food poisoning from the eatery. Although, I admit I was tempting fate by ordering pork enchiladas.

A locally owned burger joint took my favorite burger off the menu. That was Strike 1. And on that same night, the guy at the counter asked all my kids if they wanted fries with that. Strike 2 because potato chips came free, but fries were an upcharge, which the kids didn't know, so the meal ended up with us swimming in three extra orders of mostly uneaten fries that added about $10 to the bill. Not cool.

A fast-casual eatery took my favorite salad, one featuring spinach and goat cheese and a yummy warm pancetta dressing off the menu. When I noticed it was gone, I wrote an email that was both funny and heartfelt and I thought for sure I'd hear back and that salad would make its triumphant return. Nope. Never heard back and I periodically check the menu online and since there's still no sign of anything remotely like that dish, I haven't returned.

My longest grubge harkens back a good 13 years. We took No. 1 and No. 2 — No. 3 didn't even exist — on one of those rare nights out to dinner to a popular Italian chain eatery that doesn't take reservations.

No. 2, barely 2 years old at the time, was already melting down by the time we were seated at the table because that is what toddlers do. It is their special gift, along with licking the snot that runs down their faces when they have colds. Definitely not one of their more charming behavior traits but, spoiler alert, they have no charming behaviors at that age.

The chance to color on the paper tablecloth with crayons helped ease some of the crankiness. Then, the people seated at the table next to us kindly offered their high chair since they were headed out. Hallelujah!

No. 2 fussed about being put in it, and had just settled down, when a server came rushing over and demanded the high chair.

I explained that the people at the table next to us let us have it and we did need it.

No, there's a list, the server said. I pointed out that we were on the list, too.

Nope, we could get one when it was our turn. This chick was not backing down.

Though I really wanted to fight her (and I would have kicked her scrawny, perky 20-year-old ass), I instead pulled No. 2 out, who immediately began kicking and screaming, behaviors that continued throughout the meal, much to our delight and to that of everyone dining around us that night in the restaurant whose name I won't divulge but it rhymes with Facaroni Phil.

Bottom line: With all the places I won't eat at, it should be a lot easier to drop the 5 pounds I want to lose.

Life Lesson No. 237: Don't ever eat tortillas in a Seattle restaurant...Unless, that is, you like the taste of disappointment.

An Ode to Homer Simpson, or Mmmmm, Doughnuts

I love doughnuts.

They're basically full-on frosted cake but because of skilled marketing, they are legitimized breakfast food. What could be better?

So, it didn't take a lot of convincing for me when No. 2 wanted to make a Krispy Kreme run over the weekend. Of course, it was Monday when she suggested it. And then I heard about it Tuesday, Wednesday, Thursday and Friday, approximately 357 times, every hour on the hour of each of those five days. By the time we were actually climbing into the car to get the icy Oreo latte-frappe-milkshake-masquerading-as-morning-coffee thingie that she had seen somewhere and had been craving, I was not in the best mood.

I was exasperated and done. At 7:30 a.m. on a Saturday. Not a great start to a weekend.

And because I like to torture my children, I make them do the ordering when we go places. They have to tell the In-N-Out guy to leave the onions off the burger, they have to ask store clerks where to find something they're interested in, they have to ask for a price check if something's not marked. It's good for them. Puts hair on their chests.

So, when we walked into the sugary palace of delights, No. 2 — who had been saving up her money for this special doughnut-n-drink run — knew she had to order. She zeroed right in on her favorite old-fashioned chocolate doughnut, and added a chocolate-glazed for good measure, but paused when it came time for that coffee milkshake slushie.

"Tell her what you want," I urged impatiently.

She scanned the menu and a look of confusion crossed her face but she asked for an iced latte.

"Really?" I asked.

That did not at all sound like what she wanted. And, when the girl slid the pale, icy cup toward No. 2, it looked nothing like the kind of blended drink she likes that barely contains coffee but ODs on sugary add-ons. This drink had no whipped cream, no pulverized Oreos floating inside, no visible sign of a cup and a half of chocolate syrup.

"Uhhhh…"

The young woman at the counter proceeded to ring up the total.

"Is this what you want?" I asked, already knowing the answer.

"It's not on the menu, but I saw it on the website," No. 2 said, digging at her fingernails.

"If it's not what you want, you have to speak up."

My icy, annoyed heart began to thaw as she struggled to verbalize what she wanted. She'd seen this drink advertised but couldn't find it on the store's menu up on the wall.

"Can you find a picture of it?" I asked.

No. 2 grabbed her phone, tapped at the screen and produced a photo of the Holy Grail of Fake Coffee Drinks.

"This," she said and held out the phone for the cashier.

"Oooh. OK," the cashier said, cheerfully.

"Thank you," I said and No. 2 wandered off, picking at her non-existent nails, to watch the doughnuts drop off the conveyor belt until her real drink was ready.

"Thank you," I said again, appreciatively. "I'm really sorry for the confusion."

"Oh, no problem." The young woman behind the counter was maybe 20 years old. Her dark hair was pulled back and she wore glasses and a serious expression. She leaned forward and said, in a low voice, "You know, I suffer from anxiety, too. It was really bad when I was young. Really bad. I had such a hard time, my parents didn't know what to do. But, it gets better. I feel like I have it under control now. So, don't worry."

Because I am a big, squishy baby who cries at anything, I could feel my eyes well up.

"Thank you for telling me that," I said, overwhelmed by this kindness. It was all I could do not to reach over the counter and hug her. Personal space be damned.

I was so blown away by this stranger's sympathy and vulnerability and how generously she offered a glimmer of hope to someone she didn't even know.

We climbed back into the car, and No. 2 dropped her receipt onto the console. I glanced at it — there was no charge for the doughnuts.

Actual tears did fall when I saw that (I do love a bargain). I didn't think anything could be sweeter than a glazed Krispy Kreme.

Doughnuts definitely count as soul food.

Life Lesson 457: Always be prepared.

So say the Boy Scouts.

They're right. But being prepared means different things to different people. Me? I say preparedness is chocolate-chip cookie dough in the freezer, able to be baked at a moment's notice, and a barf bag in the glove compartment of the minivan. The two are unrelated.

Cleanliness is Next to…the Last Thing on My To-Do List

I don't know what jerk said cleanliness is next to godliness. But, I have no doubt it was a dude who said it — and also, I would bet any potential book royalties that he was not the one who had to clean his house.

Can you tell by my snotty tone that house cleaning is not my favorite? Of course, if you could see the cremains along my baseboards, you'd already know that.

And know that I'm not so good at it.

No, I'm not the greatest housekeeper. But then, why should I be? Socks get stuffed behind chair cushions, toothpaste gets smeared all the way over on the toilet. When someone removes a bloody Band-Aid do you think it goes in the trash? Heck noooooo, it gets left on a metal box jump, a Christmas present intended to help our two athletic children improve their verticals but which is now used mostly as a dumping ground, or as it's known in some families, end table.

Dare I bring up the discovery, many years ago, that one of our artistically inclined but gross children finger-painted a Wall of Boogers next to the bed? Our very own Pickasso. Never mind that a congested-family-of-seven-sized-box-of-tissues was within arm's reach in the other direction.

So, there's really not a lot of reason to expend a lot of energy on cleaning when there's so clearly a lack of appreciation.

I may tell my kids to give 100 percent to everything they do, but I average about 35-40 percent effort when it comes to house cleaning, just enough to keep the health department off my back.

One of the more embarrassing moments when this was evident to others outside the gene pool was when our teenage neighbor, who was going to keep an eye on our house for the week, came over to get the lay of the land. As I was talking about what we needed him to do, he slowly swiveled his head, looking all around the house and then he — a teenage boy, I remind you — said, "Yeah, and maybe I could even clean up for you."

Ouch. Oh, the shame.

A close second was when the kindergartner down the street popped over for a play date and commented on how when she took her shoes off, our floor felt like the beach.

"There's so much sand," she said, wrinkling her nose.

"Well," I told her, "you can pretend you're at the beach, oooorrrrr you can put your flip flops back on and go home."

When we moved into our repo house, the back bedroom looked like someone had been executed there. Red is not a good choice for a Jackson Pollock-y paint job. The carpet in the bedrooms was brand new and…lavender. The floor tile was so horribly filthy that it was going to cost thousands of dollars just to clean. Being broke, from just buying a house, we opted instead to pry those tiles up and throw them out. Honestly, I don't know why more homeowners, with kids, don't opt to live with just the foundation-slab concrete.

Talk about liberating.

Sure, the plain gray concrete imbued our house with all the ambience of a Costco but spill something? No biggie! Hey, call the dogs! They'll lick it up. I gave away our mop.

Since we live in a place that gets surface-of-the-sun-hot in the summer, the kids would ride their bikes through the halls or roller skate. For a time, a toddler plastic roller coaster was set up in a long hallway.

Alas, our low-maintenance lifestyle wasn't to last.

As we saved up enough money, we tackled project after project.

Guess what? Having nice things kind of sucks because now you have to care. So when a nearly 90-pound dog, scared of the vacuum, jumps up onto your nice, cherry-wood entertainment center and scrambles across it, scratching it to hell with her nails, it's a real bummer.

We did finally slap down some tile and carpet over that concrete floor. Our carpet once, for about a minute, maybe two, appeared the lovely speckled beige that it first looked when it was unrolled in our house. It's probably 10 years past when it should have been replaced. Now, the time has finally come to do it and I'm scared. Very scared.

Although, I hear dirt floors are a thing. Maybe we should go that route. With all the sand, we're probably already halfway there.

Truth: No. 1 told me she wanted an ocean theme for her bedroom. I didn't realize she was going to create her very own Great Pacific Garbage Patch.

Vroom Vroom…Said No One Ever Who Drives a Minivan

This much is true: No one grows up hoping to drive a minivan.

No one.

When I was a kid and "Wonder Woman" was my favorite, favorite TV show, my dream car, of course, was what she drove — a Mercedes Benz 450SL convertible.

Reality: My first car was a 1971 Ford Galaxy 500 that my parents bought when I was born. And then kept.

The doors on that American-made beast were so heavy, they could sever any limb caught in them. It was so big and long that not only did I miserably fail the parallel-parking portion of the driver's test but when I drove that very same car off to college, people swarmed the dorm-room balconies, hanging over the railings, to watch and see if I could actually maneuver that boat between the lines of a parking space.

Up next was an old Buick Regal I insisted upon pronouncing "ree GAL" and then the cute, small car I'd always wanted: a brand-new, white Honda Civic that was great — until I lost 10 points off my IQ every day smacking my head against the low roof while buckling a newborn into a car seat in the back.

"We need something bigger" is something I never thought I'd say after the submarine-sized rides I'd captained over the years.

We swapped the Honda for the nicest car I've ever owned, a tricked-out Eddie Bauer Ford Exploder with a six CD changer and cushy, tan leather seats that totally cradled your tush and had warmers. All well and good until we had a second kid on the way, and then it was a budget buster. Sayonara, 'Sploder and hello dependable, very blue (the shade would best be described as "electric bluegaloo") Isuzu Trooper that was basically a refrigerator box with a steering wheel and tires. I adored that thing.

By the time No. 3 was on the way, there was no more avoiding it. A minivan was in our future. The ultimate ride of passage.

I had no choice but to accept that my next car would be a super practical vehicle with magic sliding doors that shouted to the world "I change diapers and probably have someone else's boogers somewhere on my shirt!"

And, I knew what this would mean: I would have to dress slutty to compensate for my sensible mode of transportation.

People talk a lot of smack about minivans, I'm looking at you, cousin Katrina, who told the Facebook world that even though she now has a second kid: "I would never get a minivan. As much as they are super functional, life as I know it would be over."

Guess what? I'm on my second one, and I haven't yet lost my will to live. At least, not completely.

I think car manufacturers need to do us all a favor and quit — as they say — polishing the turd.

Enough already with the high falutin' names like Odyssey. You're not fooling anyone, Honda — the people who drive this car are going to soccer practice, not some epic adventure that lasts years. (Although, if you do have to sit and watch soccer practice, it will feel like years.)

Let's just call these blobby vehicles by names that are more appropriate, say, the Kia Beluga or the Chrysler Orca. That actually makes them sound kinda cute.

'Cuz here's the thing: We're stuck. We parents are practical people and we do what needs to be done. For all the mocking of the mini that goes on in social media, there are an awful lot of them on the roads and in the parking lots.

They're typically silver and look exactly like my car. Every day at Target or school or the grocery store, wherever I happen to be, there are matching minivans. I regularly hold my key fob out to the wrong vehicle, only to hear van doors slide open two aisles away.

The worst, though, was when on a family outing, I dashed into a store while everyone waited in the car. I came skipping out to the parking lot, swung open the door and as I prepared to slide into the passenger side, immediately noticed the lack of dog hair and smushed Goldfish ground into the gray carpeting. Where were the banana peels? The used Kleenex stuffed into every open compartment? And this car…this car did not smell. Once, I sniffed something so foul I was afraid I'd forgotten a carpool kid whose body was now decomposing way back in the third row. Turned out No. 3 left half of a Muscle Milk in the cup holder to ripen. You know how the tagline in those car commercials is "Love makes a Subaru a Subaru?" Well, extreme apathy makes a minivan essentially a rolling Dumpster.

This van was way too neat to be mine, I realized as I looked up to lock eyes with a surprised woman who was most definitely not my husband, sitting behind the wheel.

"Whoops! Wrong minivan!"

Yeah, I drive a minivan and so do lots of other people. So what? If you looked in the back of it, you'd say, yeah, those people know how to have a PG, tween-years-level good time: There's red confetti from the goodie bags of some recent sixth-grade birthday soiree, a shirt advertising our orthodontist that scores bonus points toward prizes if you wear it to the office, "Big Nate" books, "Simpsons" DVDs and empty In-N-Out shake cups.

Minivans are the new mullet: All business in the front and party in the back.

Take it from my wise-beyond-her-years 17-year-old: "I don't know why people care what kind of car they drive," No. 1 said, after surveying a fancy car I'd just pointed out to her. "What does it matter what kind of car you drive? You just need to get around."

Amen, sister.

Truer words have never been spoken — by someone who is looking to attend a high-priced college and knows that a nicer car would cut into that education fund.

Truth: A lost sippy cup, half-filled with milk, abandoned for about a week in 100-degree plus temperatures smells like a mixture of rotten eggs, dirty diapers, sweaty socks, fish reheated in the office microwave and…utter defeat.

A Permit to Parent

A good decade before I became a parent, I saw "Parenthood." Loved it. Still do. It stands the test of time and is one of the best movies ever. IMHO.

It speaks the truth. One of the movie's classic lines: "You know, Mrs. Buckman, you need a license to buy a dog or drive a car. Hell, you need a license to catch a fish! But they'll let any butt-reaming asshole be a father."

Oh Tod, you're very right. And so eloquent in a barely-made-that-PG-13-rating way. Well, I say, enough is enough. We need to start requiring a test not once there's a bun in the oven but earlier than that, like a permit test, to see if a person is even ready to tackle the mere act of contemplating kids.

Consider this your practice mini quiz:

1.You're at a party at someone's house and your 4-month-old baby starts to spit up*, you…

    A. Do nothing. It's a party, people expect there to be trash and vomit.

    B. Spread a paper napkin on your lap and hope it's in the right spot so your new jeans don't get ruined.

    C. Figured this could happen and have been carrying around an empty red Solo cup to catch any spewings.

2. Babies are the most slippery…

    A. Wait, I have to touch one with my bare hands?

    B. When pee leaks out the poorly applied diaper you just changed.

---

* At a party once with our infant daughter, a friend — whose nickname is The Rabbi, so that already tells you something about his goodness — was nearby as I sat with our daughter on my lap. She made that sound — as distinctive as a dog preparing to barf onto the carpet even though he's mere inches away from the tile at 1:30 a.m. — that she was going to spit up. I was still trying to figure out what to do when The Rabbi thrust his hand under her chin and caught the spit up, of a child who wasn't even his, in his bare palm. Now there's someone destined to be a parent. Also, we never see him anymore.

   C. After a bath, after a bottle, while they're being changed, pretty much all the time. You have to constantly be careful when holding them.

3. It is night. A vehicle on the street passes with its high beams on. This doesn't really affect you because you're stuck in the house at 8 p.m. on a Friday because you have a baby. You…

   A. Cry. Then sprint outside and flag down the car. The dogs'll watch the kid. The baby's asleep anyway.

   B. Watch out the window wistfully as the lights fade in the distance.

   C. What car? You passed out on the couch at 7:30 p.m. from fatigue.

4. To see if anyone or any car is in your blind spot, you should:

   A. My rearview mirror hasn't been duct-taped back up yet.

   B. Adjust your mirror and look carefully.

   C. Use the eyes in the back of your head.*

---

* My son once climbed onto the chair with me, squeezed behind me and then proceeded to pick through my hair like a monkey. "What are you doing?" I asked him.

5. If you are already in an intersection to turn left and the traffic light has changed to yellow — and your 5-month-old is buckled, rear-facing, in a car seat in the back — you should:

> A. Wait, how is the kid rear-facing? You can't buckle into the custom-upgrade Corinthian leather seats in my Ferrari that way. Do I have to get different seats installed? That sucks.
> B. Continue your turn to the left.
> C. Turn left and pat yourself on the back for having made sure six months ago that that car seat was installed by a professional* because now if you

---

"Trying to find the eyes in the back of your head."

Because of course, I told him once that I had them when he wondered how I knew he was up to some shenanigan.

* I'm always right, and one of the times my husband graciously admitted it was when I made him go with me to a fire station with our newly purchased car seat and had the resident car seat expert show us the right way to install it. A pool noodle was involved, and she and my husband were both in the back of my little Honda, hunched over and mightily tugging on seatbelts. It was surprisingly involved. He agreed that he would not have done it correctly.

get hit by an oncoming vehicle in the middle of your turn, your baby is snug and secure.

6. Which of these statements is true about changing lanes — and going from coupledom to parenthood:

    A. It's...stickier?

    B. It's challenging.

    C. It's tough and you have to be careful. But, it's rewarding and life-affirming and...super expensive. (Still worth it.)

7. If your engine dies as you pull around a corner, the best thing you should do is...

    A. Call the Mercedes dealer and chew out whoever answers the phone. This is unacceptable.

    B. Steer to the right of the road and stop.

    C. Steer to the right of the road, stop and don't plan on buying a replacement vehicle any time soon because car payments are expensive and you have college to think about.

OK. Pencils down. See? That was harder than you thought it would be, wasn't it? Yeah, now imagine actual parenting.

To score your quiz: Give yourself no points for every A answer, 1 point for every B answer and 2 points for every C answer. Yes, this is a low-scoring quiz. This isn't about math, we're READING for heaven's sake. It's a book.

0-2: Yeah, actually, you might want to consider moving back home with mom and dad.

3-7: Not bad, not bad. Maybe start with a naked mole rat, but you've got promise.

8-14: Taking a wild guess that you already have no social life — or if you do, you tend to be home by 8 p.m. Definitely, take the parenting plunge.

Killer Band Names (in my opinion):

- Awkward Autocorrect Experience
- Flaccid Cactus
- Executive Sandwich
- Unfortunate Taco
- Sarah in the Lurch
- Forced Rejection
- Getting Rid of the Tinas
- Phone Full of Jennifers
- Permanent Ponytail
- Crookshank's Revenge
- Joyful Lunacy

- Dinner Fingers
- Psychic Juices
- Minimal Drama

Cue up Huey Lewis, Time to Get Back in Time

So, we hit my husband's 30th high school reunion this past weekend.

I always have fun at his reunions. At the 10 year, I swiped an unclaimed name badge and pretended to be the high-haired girl in the pic. Who looked nothing like me, by the way.

"NO WAY! You two got married?!" one former classmate shrieked.

I nodded proudly.

I figured it would be quite the scandal this year when he showed up with me — his second, trophy, Pilates-toned wife. At least, that's what I hoped people would think. I couldn't possibly be as old as all the middle-aged looking people around me because on the inside, I still feel like the insecure teenage girl who doesn't want to smile too big and reveal that her mouth is full of metal.

Sadly, there were no unclaimed badges to steal this time around. Instead, I had a blank sticker to fill out. I figured my name didn't really matter and so I drew a fat arrow pointing one direction and wrote "With Him." Fun and interactive! Depending on which side of me my husband was on, the meaning would be totally different.

Reunions are so weird. There are people you haven't seen since you were 18 — and no one is a fully formed person at that age. Nothing illustrates the passage of time more than catching up with an almost 50-year-old you've known since kindergarten. Lots of changes. Hopefully. No one should still be eating boogers and glue at this stage of the game. Who'd gotten chubby and gone bald was the opening topic of conversation for my husband and his buddies. Which just shows that no matter how old they are, high school boys are always high school boys.

I intentionally avoided the tribute table for all those who'd died. The poignancy of lives cut short hit home all the more since senior yearbook photos adorned the swatch of purple cloth, every one of them so young and full of life. Three decades later, the class of 1987 is all too aware the clock is definitely ticking.

Flitting around the Doubletree ballroom felt a lot like circulating at a work function, making small talk and finding out who did what and how many kids everyone has.

I was amused by my husband's revisionist history of our relationship:

"This is my wife, Kristen. Yeah, we've been married 27 years."

Uh, no. Try 22.

"Yeah, we met at the newspaper where we worked."

Strike 2. We met in college. I couldn't wait to hear how many kids we had.

The food was bad but the company was good and afterward Joe was happy that he'd gone and marveled how his classmates had grown up to become a property manager, a stay-at-home dad, IT specialist, data storage manager, even a candidate for governor.

"I never would have figured people would be doing some of things they're doing," he said.

Well, no, of course not. No one ever thinks they're going to graduate, land an 8-5 job and tool around town in a minivan. At 18, you're going to conquer the world — because you no longer need a stinking hall pass to go to the bathroom.

Those skinny kids with the teased hair sprayed into submission to the detriment of the ozone layer have settled into middle age and now have kids old enough to tackle adulthood. Crazy. That was us...

In some ways, it feels like several lifetimes ago and yet at the same time, it could have been yesterday.

A snippet of my saved songs on Spotify:

- Don't Stop Believin', Journey
- Bust A Move, Young MC
- How Far I'll Go, from the "Moana" soundtrack
- Crash Years, The New Pornographers
- Baby Got Back, Sir Mix-A-Lot
- FourFiveSeconds, Rihanna
- Follow Your Arrow, Kacey Musgraves
- My Last Yeehaw, Cowboy Troy with Big and Rich[*]

---

[*] Pretty sure this is the song that got me my very own Spotify account instead of sharing one with the hub, who is horrified by my musical choices, as are my children. But dude, how could I not? This is the unholy union of country and rap and manages to rhyme "seesaw" with "meemaw." I repeat, meemaw. That's sheer awesomeness. By the way, meemaw, according to one of my children, is Spanish for mom.

- Drive By, Train
- Feel It Still, Portugal. The Man[*]

---

[*] Yes, that's the band's name — Portugal. The Man. There is a period in between Portugal and The. I get so confused by the alt indie songs that No. 1 likes because the band names and song names really do seem interchangeable.

An Inconvenient Poo

Al Gore had global warming, his "inconvenient truth." A more pressing issue in my little world?

An inconvenient poo.

It's continued to be an issue even now that I'm into nearly two decades of parenting. Never fails — someone always seems to have to go when we need to go.

Now I will admit, it was totally my bad during our first go-round of potty training that No. 1 lingered way too long on the throne. I encouraged her to bring a book — which turned into a pile of them. Yes, this totally buttfired, er, backfired.

Did not do that with the next two and yet they still manage to spend as much time in one single visit to the bathroom as I do in a month, and that includes grooming. Moms, you can relate. There's no time for a leisurely dump with a People magazine rolled up in your hand. You're in, you're out and on to the next thing. Am I right? We all know I am.

My younger two children do not believe in this philosophy. No joke, I've actually had to make multiple trips to school because one was still in the bathroom and COULD NOT BE HURRIED.

An inconvenient poo even resulted in a vacation parking ticket because No. 2 needed to go No. 2 RIGHT NOW and it took longer than the allowed 15 minutes in the loading — or, in our case, unloading — zone.

I've never been great at physics — or actually, even taken it — but in my daily life, I see how Sir Isaac Newton was right: An object in motion stays in motion while an object sitting on the toilet means you'd just better go ahead and reschedule.

And just because we're out and about, doesn't mean things won't come to a screeching halt for a bathroom break, which is super frustrating because I always do my motherly doo-ty and ask if anyone has to go before we even leave the house. As someone who is not a public pooper — never, ever have been, I prefer the privacy and relative cleanliness of my own home commode — I cannot understand why public restrooms are so…poopular. I am an admitted germophobe, and it creeps me out so much. Yet No. 3 has always been game to go no matter how sketchy and nasty the facilities are, including park bathrooms and once, oh dear God, a Porta-Potty at a soccer tournament.

I still flush with embarrassment when I think about one mortifying bathroom break in particular.

At the time, one of the medical professionals in our life was a neuropsychologist (yes, it's as expensive as it sounds) who worked out of her immaculate, all-my-children-are-grown home in a gated, resort community. On this particular visit, I just needed to pick up some paperwork. Naturally, No. 3, who was 7 years old, had to poop the minute we walked through the door.

He politely asked to use the bathroom and we sat in the office and chitchatted while we waited. And waited. And waited. Picture those scenes in the movies where everyone runs out of stuff to talk about and the clock hands seem to slow and then just stop moving altogether. Pretty sure that quick 5-minute trip stretched to 50 minutes. Horrifying.

So last year when No. 3 found out his sixth-grade trip to Colorado would be on a charter bus — complete with bathroom — he actually chuckled a maniacal little laugh like a supervillain whose only real power is the ability to poop anywhere and feel no shame. No bashful bowels on that one.

"Dude," I pleaded. "Please don't poop on the bus. Please. That's only for emergency situations. They're making bathroom stops. You can wait 'til a rest stop."

I think he may have actually tented his fingers together, a la Mr. Burns on "The Simpsons," and laughed at me.

I missed that kid terribly the four days he was away at the archeological center a state away, but the first thing I said when I saw him, "Please tell me you didn't poop on the bus."

"I didn't."

Whew. Score one — and pretty much that's my sole parental victory — for me. And, it goes without saying, one for those captive kids and teachers on the bus.

Truth: One day, when the kids were really little, I thought it would be fun to sing everything for an entire day instead of talk. Things petered out around noon, if I remember correctly. Everything I sang was to the tune of ABBA's "Honey, Honey," which is surprisingly versatile. It's really too bad that "Hamilton" wasn't around then. Bet we'd have made it to 3 p.m.

That's My Boy

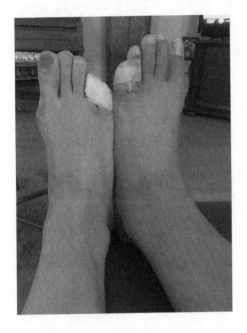

I snapped the picture because I thought it would be funny. Instead, it almost made me cry.

The image showed two feet, one left, one right. The smaller toes on both tootsies are buddy-taped — I love that description — together because the pinkies were broken.

What are the odds my youngest child and I would break our pinky toes just a week apart?

I zoom in on the photo, survey my blue toenail polish, chipped and growing out. The foot up against mine is so big. Dirty nails that need to be clipped. The medical tape is also grungy, smudged with dirt. The toes extend past mine, dark hair carpets the leg.

This is my son's foot. My 12-year-old boy. My baby.

There was a time that he himself was buddy-taped to me. So long — and yet not so long — ago.

We started as a family of four, had two girls almost two years apart and didn't find out what we were having before either of their births. I distinctly remember holding No. 2, our second daughter, in the hospital and my husband smiling, saying, "This feels right. Two girls."

We were happy.

But, I'd always liked the idea of three kids. I don't know why. I just did. Something about that odd number.

I didn't push it. I figured that was that.

Then a few years later, my husband said that you don't regret the things in life you do, you regret those things you don't do. That was his pitch to get lucky that night. He was ready to go for a third kid. We no longer had anything — no strollers, no crib, no baby car seat — but I was still game.

Though we didn't care if we were having a boy or a girl, on this our bonus go-round, we decided to find out the gender anyway. Why not? Do something different.

The girls were with us as my OB squirted blue jelly onto my huge belly. That loud and fast watery whooshing sound along with the fluttery heartbeat flooded the room.

"You're having a boy!"

My husband beamed. I actually felt a little… disappointed.

I knew what to do with girls. I had two. A boy? Wouldn't that be weird? Odd man out. And then I realized, oh, we're gonna get peed on.

His birth wasn't easy. My doctor told me later that she was actually going to have me reach down and help deliver my little boy, my son. But, things had gone awry with the epidural. It was too high. I had trouble breathing, my chest was quasi paralyzed. But good news! My boobs didn't feel a thing! Back came the anesthesiologist. The second time seemed to work better, I could breathe anyway, until I realized too late that I could feel down there…Dammit — I could feel! Every push sent waves of pain. I was in no mood to help deliver my own child. I am pretty sure there was one point when I was yelling that we should just leave him in.

At 8 pounds, 11 ounces — most of that head — accidental natural childbirth wasn't the most pleasant experience, but I survived. When his room is a mess or I have to wait an extra long time after school, I make a point of reminding him of this.

Two big sisters meant constant attention — and germs. That little dude got his first cold when he was barely two weeks old. He wasn't even a month old when RSV, respiratory syncytial virus, attacked. He wheezed, every breath crackly like tissue paper. Had he not been such a big, otherwise healthy boy, he'd have been hospitalized. Instead I brought him to the doctor for regular breathing treatments and spent two solid weeks, day and night, sitting straight, upright in a chair, his body pressed against mine, so he could breathe easier.

Perhaps it was that initial beginning that led to the little dude always wanting to be held. Always. We have video of the most amazing, pathetic weepfests — arms held straight up, bottom lip quaking with anger — where he was just begging to be picked up.

When he was old enough to sleep in a big boy bed, the early riser would get up and toddle into our room. I'd reach down and pick him up, tucking him into bed next to me, and we'd both get a few hours of extra sleep. My husband was not a fan of this little trick. I loved it. I was painfully aware it could stop at any time. When he turned 6, it did.

I reveled in how even when he was a little boy, not a toddler, he'd still reach up to take my hand. I felt so special.

I look at him now and we're nearly eye-to-eye. He's still not into bathing or grooming. He's not spending a good chunk of his 13th year in front of the mirror. That's cool. I'm not looking forward to the day that he'll cocoon himself in an Axe body spray chrysalis.

He's quieter now. I get mostly monosyllabic answers about his school day. It's not enough to ask "How was your day?" I have to specifically inquire, "What was the best part of today?" Even then I'm not guaranteed much of an answer.

It's harder to talk to him, unless it's basketball-related, which puts me at an extreme disadvantage of saying something meaningful.

His big sisters have influenced him over the years. They won him over to Care Bears and pink when he was 3. I'm hoping it means he'll be more in tune with how to treat girls, that is, once he decides they're not totally gross.

It always takes boys longer to decide that. The girls, though, already are circling. They send texts and try to hang out with him after school. In the car on the way to his first middle-school dance, I told him if any girl asks him to dance, just do it. It doesn't mean anything. Doesn't mean she wants to be your girlfriend or get married, she just wants to dance. With you. And, it should be an honor that someone wants to dance with you.

I told him how I summoned up all my courage to ask cute, shaggy-haired Darren, in his brown leather jacket, to slow-dance when I was in eighth grade. He pretended not to hear me.

His friend Steve elbowed him.

"Just dance with her, dude."

After an excruciatingly awkward pause, he did. A shuffle of shame. The last thing he wanted to do was dance with me. He only did it because his friend made him.

"Be a good guy like Steve," I counseled him, as he stared straight out the window, not indicating he was even listening. "Don't be a jerk like Darren."

He needs to use deodorant and his smelly socks make my eyes water when he takes his shoes off in the car. He burps and farts and thinks it's funny to do both and all I want to do is grab the biggest roll of adhesive I can find and buddy-tape him to my side. Or at the very least, hold his hand one more time.

People I'd love to invite for dinner:

- Kenan Thompson
- Samantha Bee and Jason Jones (but he must wear pants. He can't sit at the table in tightie whities)
- The Rock
- Stephen Colbert
- The Obamas
- Mary Roach

I'd invite author Jenny Lawson, aka The Bloggess, but I don't think she'd come because the guest list would provoke too much anxiety.

Also, after dinner — when the guests all leave — I would go out partying with Flo from the Progressive commercials.

Oh for the Love of Nerf

I found a Nerf dart the other day.

This doesn't sound particularly notable but it is because, you see, no more Nerf guns lurk in the house. Not a single one. No. 3, now a full-on, legit teenager, decided it was time. Time to get rid of them and clear out space — on the custom storage rack he and his dad built in his closet specifically for the toys — instead for his shoe collection, which now takes up all the room in his closet and his heart.

But boy once upon a time that kid loved Nerf stuff.

"Oh Mom, you have to see how cool this Nerf gun is," was a frequent comment as No. 3 online window-shopped.

For years, his Christmas lists were full of them. He asked for the Nerf Zombie Strike ZED Squad Longshot CS-12 Blaster, a bargain at $34.99, which boasted a long-range targeting scope to better zap zombies (or a poor mom caught in the crossfire of a Nerf war). He really wanted, but held out little hope for, the no-longer made Nerf Vulcan, which was only, like, the greatest, most amazeballs Nerf EVER and worked like a machine gun. True story: The vintage toy cost more than $300 when you could find it on collector's sites. How can something made of colored plastic and foam cost more than a Kia Soul? Anyway, one Christmas, that is what this kid so desperately wanted and his dad, ever the frugal one up for a challenge, set out to find all the parts and recreated this impressive piece of machinery. In the end, he probably shelled out $300, which included a four-hour round-trip drive to get one of the pieces, purchased on eBay — local pickup only. That is love. Or maybe OCD.

More than once, I was working away at my desk in the middle of the house when a Nerf war would break out around me. More than once, a forgotten piece of Nerf ammo jacked up the vacuum. More than once, I plucked foam out of the littlest dog's mouth. The darts themselves made for very good chewing, and I would guess the hard plastic piece on the end would also make an excellent bowel obstruction that would cost a pretty penny for a vet to surgically remove. Amazingly, thankfully, we never found out for sure.

I'd find darts in the couch cushions, in the window sills, behind the washing machine, in the car, they were everywhere. It drove me insane. So weird how I could spot them immediately, but No. 3 seemed to develop Nerf dart blindness to all the blue and orange pieces littering the house.

Now Nerf is no more. No. 3 has moved on. Moved on from them like he did the Bakugans and Hexbugs and like his sisters abandoned My Little Pony and Pokemon.

The other day, I was pulling out one of my shoe boxes when what happened to be wedged behind it? Something very familiar — a cylindrical blue dart topped with an orange tip. I leaned over to pick it up. I rolled the dart over in my hand, marveling at its unmarred foamness, no bite marks anywhere, as I walked over to the trash can. I popped the lid open, then closed it and instead moseyed over to my desk, dropping the dart in the top drawer. For safe keeping.

Truth: When I was a kid, I loved to roller skate and one day I noticed the wheels seemed loose. My dad fixed them. The next time I rolled down the big hill in front of our house, every wheel rolled off in a different direction.

Giving Parenting the Pink Slip

My pink slip is coming.

I can feel it.

It's very weird since this is a job I've held for nearly 18 years. But then, I always knew if I did it right — or pretty close to right — my services would no longer be needed.

That's how this parenting gig works.

It's the only job that if you do it well, you lose it.

You're not needed any more.

Oh, I've heard people say, "Your kids always need you!" I know what that really means: They always need YOUR MONEY.

It's just not the same once they move out and get that intoxicating independence, the luxurious freedom to pick out their very own hand soap.

Yeah, I said soap.

Call me weird, but what I remember most about my first apartment — and the thing that made me delightfully giddy — is that I bought my own liquid Dial hand soap. No more skanky, slimy bars that slipped off the soap dishes of my youth. Not in my place.

Then there are those people who point out, hey, you — the parent — are the one who really graduated! You get to move on and get a life of your own and do whatever you want whenever! Have fun being a couple again, maybe even reclaim rooms.

Uhhhhh what? We've just been brainwashed for the past 18 years that we have no lives of our own. I remember one date night with my husband in which we went out to dinner at a place where we actually got out of the car to order and didn't eat with sporks and when we were done in less than an hour, we didn't know what to do with ourselves. We couldn't go back before bed time, that would just be too lame. So we wandered around Costco and picked up a couple gallons of milk because neither of us had the energy level required to catch a movie with a post-7 p.m. viewing time.

Our job, for the past nearly 18 years, has been to spend all our money and time growing these fun-sized humans into full-sized ones with enough common sense to not send money to the first Nigerian prince who emails them but enough compassion to drop some change into Salvation Army kettles at the holidays. To have fun but not so much fun that they're wandering into their 8 a.m. Intro to Psychology class half an hour late, underwear jauntily askew…on their heads.

I've become very used to an incredibly chaotic, five-person family unit that never leaves me alone. Never. Not to poop, not to nap, not to work even when I tell them not to bother me because I am pooping/napping/working. So now it's just a fact of life, like the fact that someone is going to use up all the toothpaste and not tell me until after I've been to Target three times already in the past week.

At this point, I'm so screwed up that on those rare occasions when I am left alone in the house on the weekend, I feel…lost.

I have to fight the urge to drive to the nearby park and watch some other kids' soccer games. Just kidding. I'm not that crazy.

Right now, I'm not even interested in going out for a date hour, I mean, night, at all. I much prefer us to hang out, all together, relishing every minute as a family because the clock is ticking.

The calendar might say 15 years ago, but really it feels like just a few tics of my watch's second hand, that the days were so very long that I thought I would melt into a puddle of exhaustion dealing with toddlers. It's particularly cruel that just as they start to emerge from teenagerdom's anti-social cocoon and become pleasant again, they leave.

Now they've grown into cool people with relatively good taste in TV and music and food and now, now they wanna leave? Not fair.

But, I'm tough, as is true of anyone who survived the "Teletubbies" years. I'll survive this phase, too. It'll take some serious de-programming, though, to get out of my 24-7 mom mode.

Note to new parents: There's hope. Kids go through some pretty nasty stages over the years, but your kids won't always suck.

Change is hard, transitions are hard. But, they happen.

I remember how excited, and scared, I was to start college. I didn't go far — I stayed in town — but living on campus was a blast, not too much of one. I did, after all, maintain a 3.999 GPA. Still, I had a good time and made great friends, some of whom I still have today.

I'm excited for my kids to have the kind of collegiate experience that results in a near perfect GPA. And really, that is the ultimate sign of success, that your kid sprints out the front door, ready to strike out on a new adventure.

And, if we parents are lucky, our kids grow into happy, healthy people with jobs they love and pay incredibly well because I don't know about you, but I'm ready to live the lifestyle to which I did not become accustomed because all my money went to multiple rounds of braces and club sports and saving for college. Time to pay us back, kids — and that organic, orange-blossom-scented, liquid hand soap I like is not cheap.

If you are looking for a reason to buy *This.*, here it is: There's no better way to spend so little money! First of all, this book is calorie free! In fact, you will lose weight if A) you do enough bicep curls with it or B) laugh hard enough to burn a lot of calories and according to what I read on the internet, just 15 minutes of laughter a day will burn 10-140 calories, depending on a person's weight and how hard he/she laughs. Second, and even greater, it is an absolute humanitarian act to give this needy writer who couldn't find a for-realsies publisher the ultimate validation of buying my book. Also, you know you've blown way more money on dumber things so this is barely a blip. It's not even 10 bucks. You can swing it. You got *This.* (See what I did there?!)

It's Beginning to Look a Lot Like Crapmas, i.e., My Holiday Decorations Suck

Our Christmas decorations look like hell.

But, they're *my* hell. So, I keep putting them up even though they probably ought to be retired and even though I feel shimmer shamed every time a new Pottery Barn (or worse Restoration Hardware) catalog arrives at the house with the beautiful, themed decorations creating heirloom vignettes in every nook and cranny that any trust-fund child would be proud to have in his/her mansion. Imagine gold-painted twigs artfully arranged into the zombie version of Charlie Brown's beloved Christmas tree and then draped in colorful, mouth-blown Venetian glass balls purchased from the trip to Italy to celebrate lil' Loganberry Aristotle's first poopie in the potty.

Well, the "blow" part of that anyway accurately describes my stuff.

Yes, I could try and recreate the fine décor from upscale catalogs. But without the three-figure price tag of validation on the bottom, they would just look like sad DIY projects — like all my others. One year, I attempted to go full Martha Stewart and painstakingly followed the step-by-step instructions in her magazine to glitterfy a plastic gourd. It looked AMAZING. For about an hour. Then, shiny flakes began shedding. Now it's the poster child for Pumpkin Propecia. Bald spots on a fake squash are not so festive.

I have a mishmash of crap like this — almost well-done crafts and lots and lots of ornaments, fished out of after-Christmas sale markdown bins. Some stuff is Vegas flashy and some is rustic, like hand-painted village houses from my aunt who is way craftier than I. There's really no rhyme or reason to my decorating scheme. Oh wait — yes, there is: It's sheer sentimentality. I put up the Santa with the disturbing, plastic doll face and vaguely pubic-hairish white beard because my grandma bought it for me when I was born. I even still have the brown cardboard box she sent it in, with 1970 postage, to our Little Rock, Ark., air force base address at the time.

One shelf is full of "101 Dalmatians" toys that came with McDonald's Happy Meals in 1996. Yeah, that vignette probably knocked five years off my husband's life because I wanted them all so badly and we were newlyweds so he was trying to impress me so he ate at Mickey D's every day for a solid month. Speaking of solid, so were his arteries. It was only after his cholesterol cracked Homer Simpson territory that we found out you don't actually have to buy food to get the dumb toys. You can just buy the toy. Still, I appreciate his effort to this very day.

Our tree has some flashes of class — a set of a dozen, matching crocheted doughnuts and multiple jingle-bell balls in coordinated colors — but a lot of it screams DIY craft night at the homeless camp. I still have the creepster clown with Styrofoam head and a roll of Life Savers body that I've had since I was a toddler, even though the candy must've gotten wet at one point because the body is sticky and a little caved in on one side. There's the lace-covered cream ball with the beaded trim dangling off it…Wait a minute. Back up. Where is that one from? No one made it. That looks store-bought! No sentimental value to that thing. OK, that one for sure is getting pulled off the tree.

I have the picture-frame ornaments, featuring the kids frozen in time as babies and kindergarteners, all back when they were super-duper cute. Naturally I have all the ornaments the kids have made over the years: the coffee-filter snowflake, a wreath made of repurposed puzzle pieces festooned with a loooooot of glitter and beads and one random elbow of dried macaroni. There's some sort of Popsicle-stick house, scribbled with marker.

They may look like crap to you — they kind of do to me, too — but they're also memories. Good ones.

You know you're a parent when you put the noise-cancelling headphones on and you're not even on an airplane, just at home.

What About Bob?

So, we did the thing that you're not supposed to do around the holidays — we added a new family member.

My husband had brought it up before, but I'd always dismissed the idea because, well, of course I would. I'm very practical. We don't need something else to take care of, that costs too much money. We already have too many critters and kids in the house. One more thing to step over? No way.

But on Christmas morning I opened up the giant, heavy box with my name on it and — there he was. Bob. Bobsweep, to use his full name.

I felt that immediate, overwhelming rush of parental love like when each of my children was born.

What a face! As round and cherubic as a robotic vacuum can be. Absolutely, positively adorable. I mean, I do think he could use some googly eyes with long lashes but as far as functional home tools go, he's pretty fetching. Also, he never eats, never poops, never whines about how hard it is to vacuum (unlike my real children who suck at the chore and I don't mean that in the vacuumy kind of way either). No. Bob just zips around the house gobbling up stuff that shouldn't be there. It's pretty mesmerizing to watch him work.

On his first day, he inhaled a crinkly, plastic Halloween candy wrapper. Allow me to explain: The wrapper had not been languishing on our floor for the past two months. It was fresh. No. 3 got waaaay too much candy and he's very messy when he eats it.

After Bob underwent his first, full charge and was set up to roam the house, I fretted over him just like a new mom. He'd bump into a chair and I'd wince and click my tongue. "Poor Bob…"

He'd scoot under the dining room table, and it was like his first day of kindergarten. "Is he going to be OK? Can he find his way out? Can he REALLY handle all the stress, er, dog hair?"

You're not supposed to touch him or guide him, just let him do his thing but I wanted him to be as successful as he could be, so when there was a spot he couldn't quite reach, I'd kick the dog hair tumbleweeds so they landed directly in his path.

Fwwwwwip. Up they went. Sucked away.

My friend described him as staggering around like a drunken junebug. I can see that. But I like to think of him more as the little blue vacuum that could. I think he can make our house clean! I think he can! I think he can lighten my workload! I think he can!

I THINK HE CAN!

GO, BOB!

Allegedly, he even mops. Although, apparently that involves wetting a paper towel and then sticking it under him so it scoots and cleans the floor wherever he goes. That kinda sounds very similar to the half-assed method my kids use.

Bob on the first few days was, quite frankly, amazing. He'd zoom — well, not really go that fast — through the house and never got hung up on anything. He just trucked along. Nothing could deter him. Then, one day while I was out, my husband reported that Bob couldn't find his way home back to the charging station.

"Oh no. That's not good."

"It's like," said my husband, sounding dejected and disappointed by a first report card, "he's not learning."

Another day, after his scheduled noon suck run, we came home to find the rug by the front door all rumpled in a heap, and Bob was wedged in a corner, dead. His battery had run all the way down. He never made it home.

The next day, he vacuumed for just a fraction of his scheduled time. It was like he'd given up.

I know the feeling, Bob.

Then, he just stopped leaving the charging station altogether. Oh Bob.

It's never easy letting go, but at the same time, you had one job to do, Bob: suck. That's not so hard for everyone else around here.

We gave you a home, welcomed you into the family and all we expected in return, is that you keep the stinkin' floor clean.

I've seen enough sci-fi to know that the next thing to happen is Bob's circuitry will go haywire and he'll try to kill me in my sleep. Joke's on him, though. He'll totally get nailed for it because he can't even suck up the evidence.

Should you happen to have to venture into a Walmart, it will be way more fun if you play Walmart Bingo. The first person to spot, in no particular order, a butt crack, gun and pack of cigarettes rolled up in a sleeve wins! The one and only time we went (looking for a very specific type of Nerf ammo that was, of course, only available there), No. 3 got two out of three. You guess which two.

"A" Is for Anxiety

You can't fight a Type A personality. Not even in your sleep.

I know. Turns out, I'm not just Type A, I'm Type A-plus.

When I was in sixth grade, I had the toughest teacher at Marshall Elementary School. He was notorious among the older kids for grading on a curve, but bumping it higher every year so it was successively harder to get an A. I was so worried I would flunk that I never turned in any paper or test without checking it over at least three times. Mr. Mullis — who turned out to be one of my favorite teachers of all time — told me that he thought I was the slowest thing on two feet until he realized what I was doing.

And that was when I was only 11.

I didn't even know there was such a thing as a Type B personality until…just now. Seriously. I was Googling Type A and Type B popped up right along with it. Those folks are supposedly relaxed and non-competitive. I've heard of such people, but I thought we just called them slackers.

So anyway, I thought that as a working mom, if I no longer had a traditional go-into-the-office job, that would be one less stressor. Yeah no.

Instead my stupid anxiety dreams have just morphed to suit my situation.

Reporter nightmares ranged from reading lines in my stories over and over and finding mistake after mistake to interviewing sources as my teeth gradually tumbled out of my mouth.

My nonworking dream life? Much scarier.

Get this: People start showing up at my house. The doorbell rings. It chimes again and again. Over and over. Guests stream through the front door, and they are all expecting a sumptuous, home-cooked meal from me. I'm completely unprepared. I open the fridge, heart racing, to reveal an opened package of shredded Colby-Jack cheese, orange juice and strawberry jam flecked with traces of peanut butter. That's it. No, I will never, ever audition for one of those Food Network competition shows with surprise ingredients, thankyouverymuch.

Here's another one: I'm vacuuming. I run the hose attachment over the massive dog hair tumbleweeds but just as one is sucked up, another appears in its place. What the…Then, I look behind me and in a scene from an

Indiana Jones movie that does not involve exotic locales but rather a very messy house, a massive ceiling-scraping ball of dog hair rolls down the hallway at me.

Or, I'm carpooling. I'm getting ready to pull away from the school when a woman rushes up to the minivan with a girl I'm supposed to drive home. I don't recognize this kid, I don't know where she lives, Mapquest is on the fritz…

Horrifying, right? Oh, it gets weirder.

The scene is some sort of fancy gala and I'm dressed in an amazingly beautiful — and borrowed — ball gown. I really, really need to pee. I gather my full skirt and head to the nearest restroom and squeeze into a stall. I take care of business only to discover the toilet doesn't flush. In fact, it's not even functional. It is fake, a display toilet only. The skirt is splashed with urine and I panic when I realize it's going to cost a fortune to dry clean.

I know what you're thinking and no, I don't need a therapist. I can explain away each and every one of these: I entertained a lot over the holidays, my house is a pigsty with overly shed-y dogs, I carpool way too much and that last one, yeah, that harkens back to not one but two emergency plumbing calls when the toilets wouldn't flush because our main drain was plugged up with tree roots.

On second thought, maybe I *do* need a therapist.

Autocorrect says Fruity Pebbles should be "fruit my pebbles," which sounds vaguely Southern. "What in tarnation? Well, FRUIT MY PEBBLES!"

Law and Hoarder

You can't fight genetics.

It's the law, of biology. That is how I am mostly explaining away my hoarder-ish tendencies. My mom, you see, is a Grade-A hoarder. Of course, she was born during World War II in the Philippines. Her father was taken prisoner and forced to march in the Bataan Death March. My grandmother carried her and her toddler sister as they followed the route. Japanese officers invaded their home, turning it into a headquarters. After the war was over, the family grew to seven, and my grandfather spent years trying to get back what the family had lost. So, now that you know the background, you understand that my mom knows the value of a dollar and recognizes a good bargain when she sees one. It's also really no surprise that growing up, one half of my brother's walk-in closet was stacked, floor to ceiling, with toilet paper. Pretty sure they're still working their way through the stash.

Even now that it's just her and my dad in the house, she has a second freezer in the small, outside work room. Open the door, and it's deep-freeze Jenga: value packs of pork ribs and chicken breasts artfully stacked with cartons of Breyers vanilla frozen yogurt and at least one 20-pound turkey. She is the only person who can dislodge a piece without sending the entire structure spiraling onto the floor. That's my mom.

Me, I'm more of a sentimental hoarder. I've saved a lot of stuff over the years. Letters from my grandma, including one that was stuffed with $2 bills, a few from my college roommate, way-too-many stories from middle-school language arts classes and inexplicably, a lottery ticket from 2004 with four numbers circled. So maybe it was worth $5? I don't know why I kept that.

It goes without saying that I have boxes full of cards and notes the kids have given me. I've been sifting through them because No. 1 is deep in the throes of AP exams and ACT and SAT testing and I was curious about what I got on the SAT way back when. I know I have those results somewhere.

I could pay $50 to retrieve that old, archived score, but I don't know if I'm that curious. So, I keep on digging.

Awwww — found three pages stapled together of fill-in-the-blank Mother's Day trivia by No. 3 dating back to kindergarten. The pages all start out with things like "She is as sweet as" or "My mom is as pretty as" and he had to fill them in. Truth be told, they're a little repetitive, but I'm pretty proud to be as smart as "Ben Franklen (sic)." Although for the life of me, I can't understand why whoever created these sheets thought they needed to include "My mom is __ years old" and "My mom weighs ____." Seriously? That is just begging for trouble. Luckily my boy is smart and listed that vital stat as "70 pounds."

By second or third grade, his spelling hadn't gotten any better, but his creativity had progressed to the point that he was doing freestyle raps:

> This is two the best mother
>
> comeing from your daughters brother
>
> your the one who makes me happy
>
> even though this sounds crappy
>
> your the best at your job
>
> even though you shoud've named me bob
>
> your the best
>
> your even better then david west
>
> I would have picked you an outfit
>
> but my taste is a crime
>
> so I sat down and made some rymes

that was my rap

even though it sounded like crap

happy mother's day

So sweet. And way more special than a store-bought card — you can't even find something from Hallmark that uses "crap" two different ways. So special.

Hello?! What's this! Eureka!

No, not SAT scores, but a hate note. Well, technically it's a "hite" note. Angrily jotted in pencil — it sports a rudimentary stick-figure girl who appears to have a snake's forked tongue, but it's actually a line connecting to hate, er, I mean "hite" speech. The balloon connected to her downturned mouth reads, "I hite you."

No. 2 addressed it to her older sister and her friend because they made a fort out of blankets and denied her entry. It's so awesome.

"I hite you for not leding me come into your club."

The emotion in it is so raw, but time has softened it to a funny memory of those early, ultra fighty years. It's much more honest than those soft-focus family pictures where the kids arguing moments before forced fake smiles that look as sincere as Batman fist-bumping the Joker.

I show the card to them and they all laugh.

"I remember that," No. 1 says.

And that gets them reminiscing.

"Remember that time…"

Well worth the storage space. Who needs the room for extra toilet paper anyway?

I predict that the next celeb baby-naming trend will be after prescription meds…Stelara, Lyrica, Humira, Crestor, Eliquis. They do actually sound pretty cool.

The Day I Almost Died, or, the Scariest 30-ish Seconds of My Life

I thought I was dying.

For a good 30* seconds, I was. As far as I knew.

The day ahead flashed before my eyes — and I guess that should have been my first clue that I wasn't really going to kick the bucket because it was only one single day and not my whole life — but man, what a doozy: I volunteered to sign in high school students for AP exams, needed to watch No. 3's first playoff basketball game, keep score for the girls' game right after, then my pre-birthday dinner at my in-laws.

I had no time to die. And obviously, I didn't.

---

* Just guessing at the amount of time since I didn't actually clock this traumatic event.

I lived to tell my scary story…

Doesn't that line just beg for the "chung chung" sound effect of a "Law and Order" episode? I think so. Ooh, also, that would be a killer text tone. I must look that up. But, back to my near-death experience…

Unable to shake this nagging, allergy-related cough, I grabbed my husband's super-strength, prescription-only cough medicine — a leftover from a recent virus — and flooded the clear syringe with thick, yellow syrup. I immediately squirted it in my mouth — at the very same time I was gearing up for a let's-see-if-I-can-dislodge-my-spleen hack.

It was the most epic case of going down the wrong pipe ever. Immediately, I tried to cough but my throat squeezed shut. I gulped for some air, but it sounded like a gaspy wheeze.

I could not breathe.

I slapped my hands onto the kitchen counter and felt like a goldfish flopped out of water, opening and shutting my mouth, trying for air. Nothing. Just another desperate wheeze.

Ohmygodohmygodohmygodohmygod…

This is what suffocating feels like, I realized. What to do what to do what to do…

I'd just dropped off the last kid at school, so I was alone — except for the dogs. They were all outside, soaking up the morning sun and oblivious to the fact that I was fighting for my life. Also, they're pea brains. One of them was chomping a rock.

No dog in our house is ever using her nose to punch out 9-1-1 like you read about periodically in those cheesy* women's magazines at the grocery store checkout lanes.

I noticed no cars next door when I pulled into the driveway, so I couldn't stumble over to the neighbors' house to ask for help. Was I having an anaphylactic reaction to something in the cough syrup, should I grab an EpiPen? Do I call 911? Calling 911 seemed like the right thing to do. I couldn't talk, but they'd zero in on my location, right? Hopefully that would happen before I passed out or before the lack of oxygen resulted in brain damage. Which would come first?

I dialed.

"911. What is the emergency?" asked a friendly male voice.

---

* My friend and former coworker points out that if a guy said this, it would be sexist. I say since I have the appropriate XX chromosomal configuration, it stays. Plus, they are super cheesy.

I wheezed.

"What is the emergency?" he repeated.

I wheezed again, hoping the dispatcher wouldn't think this was an obscene phone call.

One more wheeze and miraculously, my throat opened.

"I…can…breathe!" I rasped into the phone.

I apologized and explained in a barely audible croak what happened.

"I'm…OK…now," I finished.

"Do you want us to send someone to check on you?"

"No, thank you," I rasped, embarrassed and relieved. My throat still felt constricted and I could only gasp the shallowest of breaths, so I shakily drove myself to the closest urgent care where Brian The Nurse Practitioner guessed that I'd aspirated some of the medicine. He ordered me a breathing treatment and wrote two scripts, one for a rescue inhaler and another for Tessalon Perles, which sounded to me like some cool substance from a Marvel hero origin story ("Just an average mother, Kristen popped two Tessalon Perles and transformed into…SuperMom, able to inflate her lungs to 20 times the normal human capacity — and get dinner on the table in under 15 minutes"). In actuality, the stuff suppresses the urge to cough. Ho hum.

Just to show how quickly I recovered from almost dying, I stopped in the urgent-care restroom on my way out and was horrified to discover single-ply toilet paper. I kept pawing at the roll thinking that one half of the layers must've been hung up in the dispenser somewhere. Nope. Only one little thin ply. Seriously?

But, that does explain the pretty minimal $35 co-pay.

Survival Post Script: I never really accepted Brian The Nurse Practitioner's explanation for my near-death episode so I've spent some time sleuthing around the ol' internet — just call me Kristen, MD, medical detective — and the most logical explanation I found is that I may have suffered a laryngospasm. To quote my personal, private physician, WebMD, "Laryngospasm is a rare but frightening experience."

I can verify this is true.

The entry goes on to explain that the vocal cords suddenly seize up or even close and block air flow to the lungs. Check.

It can be triggered by asthma, allergies, exercise, stress, anxiety. Check, check, checkity check, check. I have suffered from these things at the same time. So I guess all that's left to say is, suck it, Brian, you misdiagnosed me. But thank you for taking good care of me — and giving me such cool-sounding drugs to keep in my medicine cabinet.

Momversation: Me: "I just realized it looks like I'm wearing pjs in public."

No.1: "As someone who's done that, I think you're fine."

The High Price of Multitasking

According to the American Psychological Association, multitasking costs.

Duh.

I knew that.

It's cost me almost $9 in the last month alone. Specifically, $8.58, before tax, if you add up the two-pack of dental floss, $4.59, and the $3.99 dog treats that I have misplaced and yet to find.

It is very possible that the dogs found the treats and ate them, packaging and all. That's exactly the kind of thing they'd do. But, I doubt anyone squirreled away the floss for their own super-hygienic personal use. I say this based on our most recent dental visits at which all the kids were chastised for their flaccid flossing.

The APA, of course, is talking about the lack of focus resulting in reduced productivity. Again, duh. It's taken me two hours to get this far because I keep thinking of other places to check for that damn dental floss. Nope. Still can't find it.

I know I shouldn't try to do more than one thing at a time, but I can't help myself. I mean, multitasking and motherhood go together. Forget chocolate and peanut butter. Here's a story I've never told anyone because it just seems way too TMI-ish. But, I'm going to now.

After the birth of my first child, I was on a tight deadline to make homemade mac and cheese for some reason or another. The baby was screaming to eat, and béchamel is every bit as needy as an infant, except it already has the milk, but you just have to stir it a lot so it doesn't burn on the bottom of the pan. So, I actually grabbed a stool, plunked down next to the stove, popped out a boob for the baby and reached up to stir the béchamel sauce for the mac at the same time.

I am woman, hear me roar. I can do it all.

Of course, for every success story, there's also a complete failure, like when I thought I would remember I had water gurgling away on the stove for dinner while I chugged along for the last 10 minutes of my workout.

I didn't remember.

I smelled smoke. Wow, I thought, I'm crushing it today. I think I'm burning up the belt on the elliptical!

Nope. The water had boiled all over on the stove.

Yeah, that cost me, too — about 15 minutes of time as I scraped that nasty mess off the glass cooktop and started all over.

Or, the time I was dialing my cell phone while licking a Popsicle. You can guess which one I pressed up against my ear.

At least it wasn't as bad as the time that I was yelling at kids for some misdeeds while making brownies. I don't remember what the treacherous trio was up to, but I distinctly recall the tragic end result of my baking: a batch of incredibly beautiful, crackly topped fudgy treats…that had absolutely positively no sugar. I opted not to tell them. Served 'em right.

Sign of old age: When you see a movie running time of 2 hours 32 minutes, your first thought is "I'm going to have to pee."

ESPN Presents ParentsCenter

Forget SportsCenter.

All it does is highlight athletes, already peak physical specimens (um, not including you, professional bowlers) who have trainers and managers and coaches to look after them and make them the best they can be and who are essentially paid huge amounts of money…to play games. Whoopdedoo.

Yeah, yeah, yeah, it's cool to make a basket at half court. And yes, being a professional sports athlete can be a demanding and difficult job but that's nothing compared to parenting.

Now there's a tough job.

And, there's no multi-million-dollar paycheck to sweeten the deal. Although, it will cost you close to that to raise the little nuggets.

You're teaching them to be productive members of society and to have empathy and be kind and helping them grow up to be non-assholes. If you ask me, that seems way more important than scoring 100 points in a single basketball game.

So I say let's have a show that highlights great moments in parenting because that's truly worth celebrating. Had I seen an episode of ParentsCenter about some mom or dad's brilliant toilet training strategies, then no doubt I would have not been late for every appointment during an eight- to nine-month stretch of my life 15 years ago when I mistakenly thought it was a good idea to let No. 1 flip through books every time she sat on the plastic toddler throne.

So, here we go, the first episode of ParentsCenter…

La la la la. DO DO do do. BUM da de dah LAAAAAAA.

(That was the theme song. Doesn't translate so well for reading but sounds totally great in my head.)

Blond guy wearing glasses and ugly blue tie, clutching a handful of papers and standing awkwardly (Side note: It would suck to be an anchor these days when everyone has to stand.): "Hi, I'm John Snark."

Woman with long blond hair and very toned arms and freakishly ridiculous stiletto heels who looks like she could easily kick John's butt: "And I'm Sasha Ravenstar-Smith-Buckley. Welcome to ParentsCenter."

Snark: "An amazing come-from-behind story today, folks. More than a decade ago, at the beginning of her career as the mom of three, no one would have ever guessed Kristen Cook would be up for MVM, Most Valuable Mother."

Ravenstar-Smith-Buckley: "So true, so true. Remember the time she forgot about the tooth fairy and took money out of her own child's wallet?"

Snark, shakes his head disapprovingly: "Did she ever pay that back?"

Ravenstar-Smith-Buckley: "Excellent question. I'm not sure, John. But, in a great come-from-behind story this mother from Tucson, Arizona, really turned it around."

Snark: "Mmmm hmmmm."

Ravenstar-Smith-Buckley, shifting her weight like her feet hurt: "Yes, John, this is truly epic. Mother Kristen Cook struck out every, single time she made dinner."

Snark: "Oh?"

Ravenstar-Smith-Buckley: "Yeah, her kids would complain bitterly about any non-pizza, non-mac-n-cheese or non-hamburger foods. So, one night when she discovered she didn't have enough of the same kind of pasta, she knew it would be a big problem."

Snark: "No doubt."

Ravenstar-Smith-Buckley, reaching down to take off her shoes: "So she mixed spaghetti and elbow macaroni and corkscrews and get this…"

Snark, waving his hand in front of his face like he smells something bad: "Whew. Ever hear of Odor Eaters?"

Ravenstar-Smith-Buckley, sneering at him before turning back to the camera with a broad smile: "Her oldest was into the Disney Channel show 'Kim Possible' at the time and so when the kids looked funny at their dinner, she told them it was called Kim Pastable."

Snark, nodding approvingly while looking down and flexing his bicep: "Clever. But really, that's nothing compared to this discipline double-header."

Ravenstar-Smith-Buckley, elbowing him to quit staring at his arm and pay attention: "Go on."

Snark: "Just a sec" — rips off his sleeves, like he's a professional wrestler, and smiles — "So, back in the day, Cook's oldest was pretty sassy. Whenever she'd get sent to her room she'd say, 'I'm fine with a timeout. I wanted to go to my room any way.'"

Ravenstar-Smith-Buckley: "Pretty bratty."

Snark: "Yessiree. But get this, Cook started giving herself the timeouts. This not only gave her a break but also startled the kids enough to quit being such little…"

Ravenstar-Smith-Buckley: "Family show, Snark. Family show."

Snark, clears his throat: "Right. So, in another move Cook started assigning that mouthy kid the worst chores, like picking up dog poop, to counteract negative behaviors…"

Snark, begins to chuckle: "Talk about pee-yew parenting…"

Ravenstar-Smith-Buckley, rolls her eyes and glares at her cohost.

Snark: "Then Cook realized that she might as well get something out of it if her oldest kid was going to continually misbehave. So, she decided to set a punishment that would" — smirks — "rub her the wrong way. Every time the oldest acted up, Cook sentenced her to give a 10-minute shoulder and neck massage."

Ravenstar-Smith-Buckley: "Those little fingers can really work out the kinks."

Snark, points his finger at RSB and clicks his tongue. She looks super annoyed: "But what really catapults Cook over the top is how in the face of a full schedule, she still manages to come through when her kids need her. How many extra trips to school did she make this year for forgotten math binders and homework and lunches?"

RSB: "Ten times?"

Snark: "At least. She has earned one heck of a Mother's Day present. Well, folks, that's it for…"

RSB, interrupting: "I get to do the signoff!"

Snark, elbowing her: "It's my turn!"

Both start talking over each other: "I'm JOHN SNARK!" "I'M SASHA RAVENSTAR-SMITH-BUCKLEY."

Both shout: "THANKYOUFORWATCHINGPARENTSCENTER!"

They start slapping at each other as the camera pulls back and the theme song plays out.

So, people, what is the big takeaway from this fake broadcast? Parenting is hard, and the way to make it up to your dear mom and dad is with gifts, really nice gifts. A thank you every now and then doesn't hurt either.

Truth: I carried each of my children INSIDE my body for 9 months and they still have the nerve to ask me to carry their crap around in my purse.

CSI: Now Airing on HGTV

A flat-screen TV flickers in the background.

Football. Just a routine game, apparently. Nothing of particular import since the only two people in the room aren't even staring at the big screen but the small ones on their iPhones eerily setting their faces aglow.

A man walks in, sinking into the down-fluffed cushions of the leather couch. He smacks at a large, square throw pillow and thrusts it behind his back.

He glances down at the couch, looks puzzled, then gently brushes his hand across the squooshy surface.

"What the..?!"

The brushing becomes frantic. He snaps on a light and sticks his face up against the cushion.

"THERE'S PEN ON THE COUCH!"

Cue the music because it's time for a new episode of dun dun DUNNNNNNN.......

CSI: Couch Stain Investigation.

In this latest installment, our forensic, er, furniture examiner immediately starts performing CPR (clean, protect, restore) on the victim, an innocent and expensive new couch with attached chaise. He assembles rags and a canister of pop-up wipes and some thick, sludgy product that promises to restore the couch to the original, unsullied luster that existed when only trained, glove-wearing artisans in a kid-free, dog-free factory touched it.

Yeah good luck with that, goopy stuff.

In an impressive show of multi-tasking, the husband furiously cleans the couch while simultaneously interrogating the two prime suspects. You never see that on network cop shows.

"So, did anyone do any homework recently on the couch?"

"No."

"No."

"Did you do any kind of writing on the couch?"

"No."

"No."

"Did you maybe sit down on the couch with a pen in your pocket?"

"No."

"No."

Neither of the perps would own up to anything, but you know one of them had to be guilty. Unlike a sneaky fart, there was no blaming the dogs on this one. No opposable thumbs with which to write.

I wish I could say this is a rare occurrence in our house that was recently outfitted with new furniture — in the living and family rooms, all the better to increase our chances of stroking out over décor disasters.

Only the week before, Dumb Dog No. 2 barreled through the living room, tail a-blazing and that furry whip knocked over a plastic tumbler filled with iced coffee — all over the new tile and the newer couch. That was fuuuunnn and especially painful.

This is why I argued against paying for furniture that costs roughly the same as a moderately loaded Buick.

"You don't understand," my husband explained. "We have to pay for college starting next year so we can't buy anything for four years — and we can't live with this furniture for that long."

So, we said bye-bye to the ripped, green leather couch and loveseat set we had since the early days of our marriage and the hand-me-down, studded sofa with the unidentifiable butt-sized stain in the middle of it. But just because you replace the furniture in the crack den doesn't mean the inhabitants automatically appreciate what you've done for them and want to turn things around and not be so darn cavalier about how they treat stuff they didn't have to pay for.

There's this really disturbing sense of entitlement these kids have, like it's their natural-born right to spill and stain.

So, unlike the real "CSI," there was no ending tying up the loose ends. Still don't know who left the pen smudge that lurks on the cushion like a small melanoma that we're "keeping an eye on."

But I do know that this very domestic version of CSI is for sure destined to be a long-running show.

To prepare me for adulthood, my dad made me learn how to change the tires on my car. He should have taught me how to use a manual wine bottle opener.

The Pun That Got Away

Now, I've written stories that weren't published. I've also tapped out some pieces that goosed people into calling and yelling at me because they were so riled. Once, in a food review, a flip comment I made about lactose intolerance earned me an online putdown of being dubbed a dunderhead.

Ouch. That stung a little.

It's OK. I got over it. Mostly.

But the thing that haunts me — still — is the story that not only never was published but was never completely written even though I had the best-worst pun in the history of, ahem, paronomasia. Guess what I just learned? That fancy, multi-syllable word means pun. Who knew? Well, I did. Now you do, too. File that one away for when you're a spelling bee contestant.

Anyway, I'd heard from a coworker about this guy who had worked in Hollywood many years ago as a bug wrangler. Interesting.

He wasn't in town but was living in the state, so that worked. It took forever to arrange a phone interview, but I persisted. I'm stubborn that way. Finally, we nailed down a time to chat.

He told me about a lot of stuff and how as a kid, he came to become interested in the creepy crawly things that gross out most of us.

He talked about how, growing up in a big city, alleyways provided the neighborhood kids with the best spots for recreation. He and his buddies haunted these alleys, despite the fact that they were full of trash and animal excrement. During a stickball game, he kicked at an old pile o' poo and all these crazy bugs, glistening like blobs of oil, skittered out from under. He watched them, entranced, as they quickly disappeared. That exact moment is what kicked off his intrigue of insects.

We chatted for nearly two hours. I had plenty of material for a story.

A few days later, he sent me an email asking to read the article prior to publication. That's a big fat no-no in the journalism biz. I politely told him it was against the paper's policy.

In return, I received a scathing missive referring to newspapers as "rags" and railing against an "ego-based policy of greatness." He also said he'd already had more than his 15 minutes of fame anyway so he didn't feel the need for any more publicity.

So there.

He didn't actually say "so there," but that was most definitely implied.

My editor and I agreed that was the end of that feature.

Too bad.

Readers never had the chance to lay eyes on a beautifully crafted piece that told the tale of how Bertrum Bugguy (not his real name) was just hanging out in an alley with his buddies when he had an…epoophany.

Truth: We moved — and I packed up salad dressing that had been expired for three years.

Snooze It or Lose It

I can fall asleep anywhere at any time.

This isn't so much a humble brag as a warning because I'm feeling pretty drowsy right now, like I might nod off this very second…………..)(#(*&#(@*&lkdjal;kehjt;lkadsjd fkl;)(&#@$)!(@*^&$_)(!*@#U%$)#)(PUadkktjrlllllllllllllll

Whoops. Well, I warned you.

It's not the first time I've fallen asleep on the job. Thank goodness I'm not a surgeon…for multiple reasons, but back to the topic at hand, my internal snooze button is all jacked.

No, I don't have narcolepsy — I'm a mom.

I've fallen asleep while reading to my kids, I've fallen asleep during movies, I once fell asleep while sitting in the warm sun at San Francisco's AT&T Park while the Giants took on the Arizona Diamondbacks and something like four grand slams were smacked during the game and I missed them. Every single one. But in my defense, baseball is really, really boring.

But probably the worst happened more than 10 years ago when I was sitting up right at a teeny-tiny, kid-size table in the middle of the afternoon playing Candyland as part of No. 2's speech therapy appointment and all of a sudden I felt a little finger poke me in the eye.

"OW!"

The speech therapist and I both jumped on No. 2.

"Why would you do that?!" I said, rubbing at my right eye. "That's not nice to poke your mom in the eye!"

"I wanted Mommy to wake up."

Busted.

It's true. I was nodding off every time it wasn't my turn. The speech therapist tried to stifle a smile. Sooooo embarrassing.

More than once, I've gone to my doctor complaining of extreme fatigue. All the requisite blood tests always come back perfectly normal.

"You're a working mother," my doctor always gently says. "That's a lot. Do I have to write you a prescription to take time for yourself?"

Noooo. But then I never quite do. Something always comes up. Usually three somethings.

I blame the kids.

Pro tip for fresh parents out there: The kids are always to blame. For everything. It's your built-in excuse for being late, why the house is messy, why you lose your train of thought after 5 seconds, wow, that's a weird expression. Train of thought? Is that spelled right, is it train or trane? But t-r-a-n-e has to do with air conditioning, doesn't it? Now I'm going to have to Google that. I'm back. Nope, it really is train. Huh. Idioms are interesting things. I am so glad English is my first language because all our whackadoodle expressions would be so hard to figure out.

So what was I typing?

Hmmm. Maybe I should start circulating some sort of petition that would mandate 20-minute nap breaks during the work day. How has this not happened yet?

It would go so far in improving workplace productivity, not to mention boosting health and wellbeing and possibly even saving money. Case in point: the $60 snooze.

I have a friend, a father of four, who came home from work in the afternoon, promptly fell asleep on his couch, and it ended up costing him 60 bucks. How is that possible? Because day care gives you a 15-minute window before you start getting charged by the minute. By the time day care called, startling him back into consciousness, to see if he was ever picking up his kids, the tab had hit $60. A bargain, if you ask me. I'd pay way more than $60 for a nap.

Crunchwrap Supreme, Naked Egg Taco, Doritos Locos Tacos. Does Taco Bell exclusively employ seventh-grade boys on its development team?

Therapy Dropout

Sometimes, you fail.

I tell this to my kids all the time and explain that it's OK because failing isn't a bad thing because you learn something. They don't really believe me. But luckily, I was able to show them a real-life example: The little deaf dog and I failed.

Big time.

For weeks we'd been training to be a therapy team. It's something I've wanted to do and with her super-chill disposition, I thought we'd be great. So the morning of the big evaluation, I anticipated what would be the hardest part — walking past another dog without freaking out over the mind-blowingly exciting possibility of contact with another canine — and took her to the park.

It was so early — because that is how she unfortunately rolls — that I wasn't showered, I left the house without brushing — hair or teeth — without a bra (not a traffic-stopper) and headed for the park, hoping other dogs would be out. I spotted some immediately and sped up so that we could get the party started. We passed antisocial ankle-biters, friendly Golden Retrievers, we had eight, separate dog interactions, and I was able to keep her attention and get her to walk on by.

Yes! We've got this.

We go to the test. She sits. She's petted and groomed by strangers. She walks along an orange line with me and then we navigate a room full of people going in different directions and with one woman ambling slowly by in a walker. A book drops loudly behind us. Nothing. (I knew she'd ace that part.)

Then, it's time for the down command. This always gets a big response at home. She typically flops onto the floor.

It's pretty darn cute.

I sign the "down" command. Nothing.

I'm allowed to circle around and try again.

Still, nothing.

"I'm sorry," the woman with the clipboard says. "We have to stop the test."

And like that, we flunked. Failed.

Everyone was very nice about it and afterward wanted to pet Lilly. They lavished her with attention. I'm not sure why because I was the one with my tail between my legs.

One woman asked if she could give her a treat. Of course. The woman signed down. My dog, of course, did it. For the treat. Pretty sure that was my favorite part.

So, all the therapy dog literature drills into you that when your dog is one-half of a therapy team, the pooch must be predictable and controllable. Makes sense. But, I think no dog can ever be truly controllable or predictable. I also think the same is true of people.

So we could test again, but ya know, we have a 50-50 chance of bombing out again.

She is sweet, sassy, playful, squishy-stuffed-animal soft and the most unbelievable pain in the ass between the hours of 4 and 8 a.m. as she eagerly awaits her morning walk and breakfast.

Contrary to what I'd pictured in my head, she's not gonna sit patiently and supportively while kids stutter out words as they practice reading at the library and she's not going to be strolling the aisles of a hospital, brightening patients' days and leaving long white hairs all over their beds.

But, she's still going to snuggle with No. 3 in the morning when he hunkers down in the almost-built-for-two cuddle chair, getting in a few minutes of screen time before school. I'm still going to take her to the school for pick up and smile as the little kids all ask to pet her silky coat. I'm still going to take her to the chichi mall where dogs are allowed in all the stores and the Anthropologie ladies will fawn over her and I'll continue to tell people who don't ever ask that my dog is deaf and she's pretty amazing and that you shouldn't shy away from adopting a special needs dog because they make wonderful pets.

This whole exercise cost time and some money, but after almost three years of thinking about it, and considering it a kind of a bucket list item, I did finally do it. That's something.

My dog and I went through therapy training, and it felt good. It was fun to hang in the park and meet new people and learn more about this funny little critter. It felt good to work toward a goal, even though the outcome was quite different than I thought it would be. Still, I enjoyed the experience of it all. And ya know, sometimes that's enough. And, in failing I learned something important about my dog: She's a turd.

Kidding. Sort of.

Vocabulary Word: *inshoecurity* (n): The inability to tell if shoes fit correctly and if you should buy them. My husband suffers from this. Don't ever shoe-shop with him. You'll regret it.

Doctor's Orders: Add Probiotics and Fiber Gummies to Your Diet

It's weird getting old.

Forget modesty or any sense of personal space. Pfft. Gone — especially if your preference is to not drop dead unexpectedly. So, we let strangers do the most personal, intimate things to our bodies. Once a year, some lady I don't know cups my boobs and maneuvers them onto a cold machine that will then smush and X-ray them. Guys get probed by a gloved finger where the sun don't shine. Not fun. Either of them.

Then there's the colonoscopy.

I have a hard time even pronouncing that the same way twice. Too many O's. Calawn-AH-scope-y, CO-lynn-os-co-PEE…It's that second one (I just checked), but I kept accidentally saying it the first way when I recently took my husband to get his plumbing snaked for the first time.

Although, really, how has no gastroenterologist tried to market this procedure as the Super Bowel? People would be so much more into it.

Because there's a family history, the hubster had to do this years earlier than usual. He was a trooper. Cleared his busy schedule for two days, bought a lot of Gatorade and clear juices and hunkered down close to the guest bathroom.

They may knock you out for the procedure so you don't feel a thing, but the prep is not so pleasant.

When No. 2 asked what exactly happens with this mysterious "little procedure" as we kept calling it in mixed company, her dad spared her the gory details. He stuck with the plain and simple "They're just going to take pictures of my insides."

We failed to synch up this bit of parenting because when No. 3 wanted the scoop, I told him EXACTLY what would occur. He listened quietly, completely expressionless. Didn't even flinch. "It's not the most fun thing you do, but when you reach a certain age, it's really important that you have it done," I said.

"I'm fine with pooping," he told me. "Plus, you get to drink a ton of Gatorade? Sounds great to me!"

That's one way to look at it.

And even though colonoscopies are normal and part of, gulp, middle age, they still remind you of the fleetingness and fragility of life. Just because I downplayed things for the kids, doesn't mean I bought my own nonchalance.

Though I sat in the waiting room, pretending to noodle around on my phone the worst thoughts bounced up and down in my brain. What if they find something? What if something goes horribly wrong? Then, my mind got progressively darker and crazier. Hey, do they reuse the tube thingie that goes up there? How do they sterilize that? What if it's not cleaned properly, have people gotten infections from that? And I thought of how my coworker told me that when she had it done, she woke up just before it was over and could feel what was happening and, worse, hear everyone having a very casual conversation about their 401Ks.

Oh dear God.

I was working myself into a full-blown lather when a nurse came through the door.

"Kristen? For Joe?"

She took me back, and the doctor greeted me, saying everything looked just fine. No cancer, no polyps. No need to do this again for 10 years.

He left and another nurse read me the post-procedure instructions, which called for adding probiotics and fiber gummies into my husband's regular diet.

I was there just in time to see him, still sedated and lying peacefully on his side, wheeled out and headed for the recovery area.

I felt relieved but also, it shattered me a little to see this person, my rock, look so very vulnerable. Because I cry really easily, I felt on the verge of tears. And now I'm going to talk about farts because I have to lighten the mood. I wondered how bad the gas side effects might be later since we'd be hanging together, for the rest of the day, at home.

While in the grand scheme of things, this was just another box to check on those health forms, now that we're grownups it felt much bigger — like a crisis averted.

When No. 3 came home, he politely asked how his dad was while heading straight to R2Fridge2, as our backup refrigerator is called because I say it must be called this. He leaned down and saw the rainbow of leftover, untouched bottles of Gatorade.

"Yeeeeessssssss!"

Even better, I never did detect any farts that afternoon.

An actual text message conversation with my husband:

Me: "Got a mole removed off my butt!"

Him, unconcerned at becoming a single dad if I die of melanoma: "Sounds like a viable 2020 GOP candidate."

My Black Son Who is Most Definitely Not "The Jerk"

With all due apologies to Navin R. Johnson, it's really my son who was born a poor, black child.

If you ever saw that classic Steve Martin movie "The Jerk," that sentence needs no explanation. But, if you're a young whippersnapper who just found this book in your mom's bathroom while you were visiting, here's the deal: Steve Martin is the adopted, super-white son of African American parents who grows up completely oblivious to his adoption. Also, it's a funny movie. At least, as far as I remember — it's been years since I've seen it.

Of course, my son wasn't born poor. Or black.

He's pretty middle-class and about the shade of a Starbucks coconut-milk mocha macchiato. But, until he was 7 — and we broke the truth to him — he assumed he was African American.

Truth be told, he is darker than both of his parents. Some friends of ours — she's half African American, he's

Hispanic — laugh at how he's darker than their own son. Another friend said she was shocked to discover I, pale as I am, was the biological mother.

When No. 3 was 5 years old and Barack Obama was elected president, he spotted the Time magazine featuring our new commander-in-chief on the coffee table. He got so excited, pointing and smiling.

"The president is dark! Like me!"

His elementary school did not have an especially diverse student population and after one of the early days of first grade, he came home, sadly shaking his head as he said, "Well, there's just two of us who are the only black kids in the class."

Later that year, on MLK Jr. Day, I was chauffeuring a carload — including No. 3's good friend Luke, who's as blond and pale and blue-eyed as can be — for some mini adventure, and I started quizzing them to see if they understood the importance of the holiday that sprang them free of school.

"If it weren't for Martin Luther King Jr.," No. 3 said somberly, "Luke and I couldn't be friends."

I still have a Mother's Day card he made me. It's carefully folded into fourths and features a black and white photocopied picture of him, his skin scribbled in brown crayon. It reminded me of a coloring sheet I'd worked on in religion class back when I was in kindergarten and lived in Guam, where most of the population was pretty pigmented.

The Virgin Mary was my subject, and I carefully colored her skin with the darkest crayon I could find, which my (do I need to mention white?) teachers found hysterical. I didn't understand why they laughed. I remember asking my mom what was so funny about my coloring job? She pulled out a children's bible and explained that most people just thought of Mary and Jesus and God as white.

I'd never thought about what color they were.

Just like how I was always surprised when new friends would see my mom and later ask, "That's your mom?!"

My mom is Filipina, which no one ever guesses when they see my very round, green eyes.

So yeah, I technically can check the Pacific Islander box on forms, and no, my son despite his Coppertone tan is not especially ethnic, save his quarter of Filipino-ness.

We don't all look the same, but we are all family — no matter that some of us are darker and others look distinctly Asian. It shouldn't make people look twice and wonder. They should just see the love. Still, sometimes I think it wouldn't hurt to steal all the world's supply of peach crayons...

Yes, I am a "mom" but I really prefer the title "unpaid children's life coach."

I Really Wanted Grape

"You get what you get, and you don't throw a fit."

This was one of those golden rules learned early in parenting, courtesy of our beloved preschool. Another brilliant tidbit was "Use your words" a phrase typically uttered when the wee ones indulged in their favorite snack: toddler tartare. One kid would chomp another kid because one of 'em was either mad or just simply a little douchebag in training. I'm sad that I never saved any "bite reports" that were sent home. Also, I've parented both chompers and chompees, and all I can say is the little nugs are gonna bite. Not a big deal.

But back to that "getting what you get" thing.

At our preschool, it referred specifically to those special occasions when all-natural, juice-only, no-sugar-or-artificial color-added frozen pops were handed out to the kids. Each munchkin received whatever was randomly plucked from the box, and you were supposed to be happy with it. No matter the flavor.

Just like parenting.

A nurse hands you that yowling bundle fresh out of the chute and you peel back the blanket to count fingers and toes. And, you exhale as you find 20. You figure it's all good.

Until it isn't.

That perfect little tot with the button nose and shiny blue eyes who was just beginning to babble suddenly stops. Off to the pediatrician! Ah, repeated ear infections are to blame. Not a problem, all we've got to do is minor surgery to put in tubes, help drain out that pesky fluid when the infections hit.

Oh, that didn't do it? Still not talking? Speech therapy it is!

Hey, and um, there could be some developmental delays going on here and it looks like, yup, yup, hypotonia, too. Oh sorry, that is just the fancy medical term for low muscle tone. Let's add in physical therapy and occupational therapy, too.

Before you know it, "What to Expect When You're Expecting" and all those cute Anne Geddes photo books move off the shelves, replaced with somber reads dedicated to dealing with the difficult/unique/special needs child.

A file for paperwork gets created. Its thickness grows even faster than the kid whose name is on it.

A glass door is shattered in a fit of anger. Now a psychiatrist is added to the mix. Welcome to the wide world of pharmacology! It's fascinating and confusing. And, oh, here's some research on different meds. Yeah, we know you were a liberal arts major who has no medical background whatsoever, so study up!

Of course the search for help and answers leads to, where else, Google — and regular panic attacks by the glow of a computer as you discover all the things that can and might be wrong and what treatments exist.

Vision therapy? Hmmm, let's go for an evaluation. No wait — cognitive training! Yes, let's try that! It's expensive, sure, but research shows it works. Don't cheap out now — this is your child.

Let's order an EEG. Ooh, now time to get on the waiting list to see a neurologist. OK, now let's schedule an appointment with a developmental pediatrician. That would be helpful.

Another label, another lengthy report. This one at least explains that impulsive behavior and non-existent attention span. But, don't worry our dependence on cellphones will make those shortcomings barely noticeable. Smart phones are turning us all into gibbons!

Wait, wait. You thought you had this all figured out? Nope. Not done yet. Look at how her nails are picked well below the quick, and she suffers paralyzing anxiety and meltdowns at the very sight of the red letters spelling out "emergency exit."

Let's bring in a psychologist. Actually, on second thought, maybe try this specialist — he handles "complicated" cases and no he doesn't take any insurance, but this is your child. How can you not pay out-of-pocket for someone who might make a difference? You have to do it.

Another label. Another thick report.

Ya know, cutting out gluten and dairy, and basically all joy, could improve things. Give it a try!

Enough. Just enough already.

Gonna be honest, I really wanted grape. Instead, I got handed lime.

Not at all what I was expecting.

And lime comes with so much paperwork and so many medical and therapeutic professionals.

Assessments, referrals, behavioral health plans, medication guides, educational assessments, psych evals, a very pricey, not-covered-by-insurance neuropsychological evaluation that was not accepted by the school district followed by the equally lengthy paid-by-the-public-school-district evaluation that did indeed back up that first neuropsych eval — but only, of course, after a very lengthy appeal process.

Stack all those highlighted, annotated sheets up and it would equal three phone books. At least. And we're not talking crummy little suburb ones but full-blown, metropolitan-area directories.

It's impressive.

It's also...disheartening.

But what can you do?

Well, to quote that great phishlosopher Dory, just keep swimming.

When you think about it, we all have challenges. I will cop to a bit of obsessiveness and a very weird phobia about handling raw meat with my bare hands and so every year at Thanksgiving, I Saran-wrap myself up to my elbows just so I can retrieve the turkey's insides that must be removed.

Some issues don't come neatly labeled or require fancy doctors, others do. And you figure out how to muddle through with your neuroses and hang-ups and just...swim. Keep that head above water.

There's no shortage of blogs or essays in which parents talk about how it's cool to have a special-needs child and how there's no way they would change a thing! It teaches everyone to be more compassionate and tolerant! Which is true, but also a load of bullshit. No one would — given the choice — wish for a kid's life to be harder than it needs to be. And I say that as someone who knows firsthand.

So, you change your idea of what the future should look like. Success is measured differently. And you cheer extra loudly for the triumphs and shut yourself in the bathroom and cry, quietly, at the recurring setbacks. One step forward, two back is never more true.

You pick yourself up and reach out for that lime ice pop and be gracious because you get what you get.

And ya know what? Lime is a perfectly lovely flavor. It just wasn't quite what I was expecting…

If the orthodontist comes out of the office and sees a shadow on your full bank account, it means six more weeks of braces.

Mr. Martha Stewart

I married Martha Stewart.

Could be worse — I could've pledged for better or worse until renovations do us part with…someone like me. Then where would our family be? In a yurt? With a dirt floor?

Which, honestly, would better suit our lifestyle that includes kids and dogs, in triplicate.

But since I do enjoy indoor plumbing, it's good to be married to someone with a flair for interior design, who can detect those subtle differences between ecru and beige because if you asked me, I'd say they're both gonna show barf stains.

I just don't have a lot of interest in that stuff and can't handle any of those flipper fixer-upper shows on HGTV. Sorry not sorry.

Part of it goes back to what I said before — kids and dogs live here. So, there's really not much point. Half-filled plastic cups of water are everywhere, waiting to be tipped. Dirty clothes pile up on bedroom floors. Sandals are abandoned throughout the house. Scruffy blankets pile on the couch. Oh wait — that's a dog! GET OFF THE COUCH.

See why we can't have nice things?

The last time I actively participated in choosing the décor of my home was when I was a freshman in high school and I had to make a time capsule that included magazine and catalog clippings to show what the living room of my future home would look like. It had gray carpeting and dark green leather couches. Lo and behold, a green sofa and love seat were the first furniture purchases we made as a married couple. As a bonus, I picked out — on my very own — a sleek mauve, easy chair with black lacquered legs and splashed with tres '80s streaks of teal and purple. My husband dubbed it the Barf Chair, so named because if anyone threw up on it, you wouldn't be able to tell.

Do you detect a theme with my interior design?

So did he.

Now he pretends to ask me if I have an opinion about whether the exterior trim is painted army or olive or cargo, but we both know I don't. Dude, they're all just green.

We bought a fixer-upper which has meant three different bathroom remodels. He's solely responsible for how nicely the sea-glass colored accent tiles pair with the Sonoran Fawn stone counter in the master bath.

With most of the big projects out of the way — OK, they're not so much out of the way as we're out of money — now he's turned his sights on throw pillows.

Good grief.

He laid out his decorating plan that involved assorted neutral tones in varying sizes. I think. What I heard was the waaah-wah-wah-wah droning of the teacher in the Charlie Brown cartoons. Lean in because I'm going to whisper this next part — I am pretty sure he created... *a Pinterest board.*

I stumbled across some pom-pom trimmed pillows decorated with cartoony cactuses online and shared with him. It did not get a response.

Over the weekend, he decided to go shopping.

"I'm going to Home Goods, want to come?"

Uh, no way, Joe-se.

So instead, my day was punctuated with texted pillow porn. Blue puffs with oversized buttons, rectangles with black-and-white geometric patterns, square ones, way-too-white ones, checked pillows provocatively placed on a chair. Lots and lots of pillows.

He ended up bringing home three. That was just for starters. Later in the week, a massive brown box arrived. I was scared to pick it up since it was definitely vertebrae-crushing size, but instead it was quite light. Guess what was inside? Yup, pillows. One ginormous one — I dubbed it King Pillow — and two for lumbar support, all in tasteful shades and textures. A few days after that, he brought home two more covered with fluffy nubbins all over that make me want to take them to a pillow dermatologist.

He lined them all up across the couch.

"You're supposed to have a variety of textures," he explained.

Is this really the same guy who buys only tan pants?

And, has he not seen what happened to all our throw blankets, which have nibbled holes and chomped-up edges? These pillows are doomed, doomed, I tell ya, but for now, today, they do look kinda cute.

The gift that truly keeps on giving? Homemade gift certificates from the kids for car washes, etc., and they forget to put on expiration dates. Rookie mistake.

Love Letters

Tucked into a fire-safe lockbox in the storage closet are all the important family documents: the license for my (first) marriage, everyone's social security cards and birth certificates and my woefully expired passport. Also stashed in that black metal box is one of my most prized possessions.

Actually, three of them.

Letters. From my mom, dad and younger brother, all folded into an envelope bearing my name in my mom's small, careful, cursive writing.

Each one professes what they love about me. It was done under duress. OK, not really, but, it was assigned homework for them: My high school religious ed teacher had the families of her students pen the tributes. Even as a 17-year-old, I appreciated what a thoughtful gift it was.

And still is.

Who doesn't need a reminder every now and again that he or she is special?

When my kids were born, I started journals for each of them. I found something to marvel at on a daily basis. I couldn't bear the thought of them not knowing my absolute, profound, immediate love for them. But here's the thing: At about three years, orneriness kicks in. Don't let anyone complain about the terrible twos, three is so much more torturous and then four is worse than that and then…

No sooner do they learn to string words together then they flip them on you and talk smack. Then, there's the extreme fatigue of growing a little human into a productive person. So all those things mean…there are a lot of blank pages in those well-intentioned journals. I tried to make entries on their birthdays, but I haven't done that in years either. Now I'm not exactly sure where in the storage closet those books are. Whoops.

Yup, the ones you love the most are the ones you also take the most for granted. Sure, you can say "good night, love you" every evening but it just doesn't have the impact of an actual, written profession that mines the exact depths of your love and also, when you write a bunch of little essays that poke fun at them, you probably should remind them now and then that they, at certain moments, can be pretty awesome. So, with that I present love letters to my family. Note: This does not mean I will not shout at you for not doing your chores or grant any special dispensation for messy bedrooms. But, I do love you. Way past the moon.

How do I love thee? Let me count the kids…

No. 1, you are the first-born. The one who quit napping at 2 years old — when I needed it most — and the sassy kindergartener who hurled insults from your car seat directly behind me at me. I remember vividly that time I pointed out the stench of dead skunk as we cruised past a wash.

"That smells like YOU, MOMMY!"

Ouch.

It's hard to wrap my head around the fact that you, who have such neat, microscopic handwriting that it looks like a font and have all these detailed, color-coded notes for school, are the same kid who leaves discarded, protective deodorant caps on your bedroom floor. One is understandable, two is just weird. Why are you collecting them? Girl, you are messy. You are also the most amazing, determined, thoughtful person I know. At almost 17, I don't know that I could have had the courage to stand up for myself and do what's right in some of the situations you've found yourself in, but you always do. You're strong and smart and have been able to overcome the hardship of two math-challenged journalists as parents to fend for yourself in calculus. A lot of parents say this but I honestly believe it: There is nothing you can't do.

No. 2, at an age when most teens are surly — not that you don't have your moments — it's so nice to hear from, pretty much everyone, how charming you are. All I do is say your name and casual acquaintances will say, "Aww, I love her. She's so sweet." Not a surprise, really, considering that you have always been a people person, always made friends with complete strangers. I still remember that time at the Costco food court, you were about 5, and you kept gravitating toward this older couple sitting across the aisle from us. The man had a big, ol' white beard so maybe you thought he was Santa? You'd flit from our table to theirs and then you came back waving a $5 bill. The couple were so smitten with you, they gave you money for ice cream.

You never tire of complaining about chores, but you do them. So, thanks for that. And, while we do get into some pretty nasty screaming matches, you always apologize later and never hold a grudge.

You've got a lot of guts, too. You wanted to go to the fall dance, even though none of your friends were going to be there, so you went and danced and had a great time. That kind of moxie will take you far.

No. 3, you leave clothes heaped in the laundry room days past when I ask you to put them away. You eat like Cookie Monster — who at least has an excuse for his messiness because he doesn't have an actual throat. You, my friend, do. And yet, you leave enough scraps in my car and around the table to give our dogs some serious chubs. I've made more trips to school for forgotten sports uniforms and homework and yet you just happen to be the most natural leader I've ever seen. You have this amazing ability to roll with anything and while you ooze confidence, you're not conceited.

I was beyond proud when another mom shared that you were nice to her son who had been having challenges navigating the tricky social circles of middle school. You were team captain and picked him first instead of leaving him stranded in his usual, last-to-be-picked position. When other kids protested, you shut them down. That was good, son. So was the time you looped in that other kid, not your favorite, who wanted in on twins day with you and your buddy. You graciously altered the outfit to include him. That is true class.

Now, could you be a better free-throw shooter? Hey, no one is perfect...

And then of course there's the husband. Seriously, can it be that hard to call and say you're running late more than two minutes before we typically sit down to dinner? You hear 10 percent of the things I tell you and your ability to remember what I've said is probably closer to 2 percent, but that's OK because you're the most supportive spouse I know. Facing the possibility of crippling college debt, you enthusiastically encouraged me to quit my job to pursue a dream.

We're very different people, but we make a great team: Look at this family we created that can be so shouty and fighty and spendy but so flat-out amazingly wonderful. I'm still not sure about your decision to let the kids watch "It's Always Sunny In Philadelphia" and "Deadpool," but I've never regretted my decision to marry you. And, I sure hope we don't hate each other when we're retired and around each other all day every day, day in and day out.

Vocabulary Word: *oppootunity* (n) When you give the dogs a chance to do their business outside before leaving them in the house for the day.

Gaining Some Perspective

At the risk of sounding like a Will Shortz puzzler, let me ask you this: What is the greatest gift that you can't actually give? Instead, it must be acquired, over the years, like the cool, weathered finish a leather jacket develops only after it's been worn through some truly rough weather.

Can you guess?

Perspective.

Something no one under 30 has. Actually, probably no one under 40.

It's the one thing I want so badly to give my kids, but they don't get it. Not even when I smack them in the face with it.

No. 1, loudly groaning: "Life is so unfair! I can't believe it's this awful! How can I have to take two SAT subject tests on the same day. That's the worst. Just the worst."

Feeling like this kid needed some, ahem, perspective, I disagreed.

"Actually, that's not. The worst would be you have a little scratch and think it's no big thing and then it gets all infected and you wind up in the hospital and it turns out it's MRSA and then all your limbs get amputated. Now that would be the worst."

Silence.

I could tell by her wide-eyed look, she was gonna be Googling "what is MRSA" for the next two hours. I probably took things a little too far, but I didn't know how else to impress upon her that life is so much bigger than two SAT subject tests on the same day.

On the one hand, that's an amazing testament to our fortunate middle-class life that this is one of her worst moments, which I think has since dropped to second place on her Suckiest Thing Ever list since a test proctor cheated her, along with a roomful of other overachievers, out of 12 minutes while taking the AP Physics test. And her school and the College Board did nothing to make it up to the poor students.

But, guess what? It doesn't matter.

Perfect GPA? Big deal. Perfect SAT score? It's just a number.

But what do kids know? They've just barely got a decade under the belt, a belt, I jealously add, that is set on the tightest hole possible because they're nowhere near 40. Those of us who've had time and lived and loosened our belts a few extra notches know some stuff.

So, what truly does matter? Well, here's what I've learned:

- It's much more important to gain knowledge than to just get a good grade. We memorize a lot of dates and facts, but that isn't gonna make it easier to fill out those 1040s one day — or to know how to cook a non-dry Thanksgiving turkey.
- It's OK to ask for help.
- Admit when you screw up and don't offer any excuses. Just say you did it and move on.
- Yes, you CAN say no.*
- Don't stew. If something's bothering you, talk it out and sooner rather than later.
- Do your best. This is not to be confused with being THE best. No one is the best, and anyone who says he or she is is really just an asshole.

---

* It took me a good 45 years to learn this one. Wish I'd picked up on it sooner.

- Try putting yourself in someone else's shoes before you judge them. If they're ugly shoes, then judge them harshly.
- Real friends don't ask you to buy something from them.
- Brownies should not be frosted.
- Keep snacks in the car.
- Don't be afraid to laugh, especially at yourself.
- Pie counts as breakfast food.
- Skip Spanx. You'll be happier and more comfortable just letting it all hang out. Plus, you can eat and not develop any numbness in your lower extremities.*
- If you have kids, don't bother buying anything nice — furniture, cars, a house. Baby poop is as toxic and stainy as the acid blood that squirts out

---

* OK so I was totally just thinking about straight-up comfort when I wrote that, but health flash! I discovered there really is something called "tight pants syndrome." People who wear clothing that's too restrictive can suffer from numbness that travels down the thigh called meralgia paresthetica, which actually would be a pretty name for a girl. Too-tight pants can also cause abdominal discomfort, heartburn AND belching. I would have to think farting would also be an issue. Even worse, if you're a dude who loves skinny jeans, you could end up with a twisted testicle that could die. Yikes. I don't even have testicles, but I'm going to go clean out my closet and get rid of my skinny jeans.

of the extraterrestrials in the "Alien" movies and whatever it doesn't destroy, the pimple medicine your teenagers use will.

- Say something nice. Pay a stranger a compliment; it will make you feel good, too.
- Be there for people. Have sympathy and empathy, have all the -pathies, except of course for the one that starts with 'a.'

Vocabulary Word: *techretary* (n) — the kid in the shotgun seat who has to answer my phone and text for me while I'm driving.

Call Me Mrs. Magoo

So, eyes are the windows to the soul, eh?

Then someone pass me a jumbo bottle of Windex because my vision's so jacked I can't see much past the uvula.

It was bad enough that I started wearing glasses when I was only in first grade. The miraculous discovery that I was nearsighted happened at the exact same time I contracted chicken pox. Thanks, Matt L. (he gave me the pox). Thanks, Dad (he gave me the bad eye genes).

Things only got worse.

By the time I was in high school, my glasses were so thick that one time, the lab made a mistake and sent back my unwhittled lenses and they looked exactly like contact lenses for the Jolly Green Giant. No joke, they were at least two inches thick at the edges.

Actually, no matter how hard those eyeglass lab techs work, my lenses still stick out way past the frames. You do not want me looking directly at you in the sun when I am wearing my glasses. I will burn a hole through you faster than Cyclops. Ants scatter when I look down.

Recently, as my friends all dipped their toes into 40, they started complaining about how hard it is to read and how they had to buy cheaters.

But I read somewhere authoritative (maybe People magazine) that as you age, you become farsighted. (If you, like me, just snorted because you initially read that as "farTsighted," then you already know what I'm talking about.) This means those of us who are nearsighted will have our eyes start to correct, to a point. This I call ocular karma*! I got so excited when I heard this tidbit, but when I asked my eye doc about it, he quickly knocked the wind out of my sails. Sorry, you'll never correct that much, he assured me.

Dang it.

Sure enough, it may have taken me longer than my friends, but I, too, no longer can make out small print. Adding to my visual woes, the vitreous — the gooey gel stuff you may remember learning about in sixth grade — in my left eye pulled away from the retina. This is the kind of thing that can happen, but to 70-year-olds. Remember

---

* Ocular karma — good band name!

when you're little and people compliment your parents on how advanced you are for your age? Yeah, this is not the same thing. No one wants to be in their 40s and experiencing things a septuagenarian does. Trust me.

So now in addition to nearsighted jankiness, I have to see through constant floaters in my left eye. Fuuuun.

I have gone from being a run-of-the-mill, straight-up four eyes to having eight. I think. Someone check my math. I now have three different pairs of glasses. And contacts.

I've got cheaters for reading that teeny font Entertainment Weekly reserves for its double issues, a night-driving pair for an extra boost AND one great-googly-moogly-my-eyes-are-so-tired-and-dry-they-stuck-to-my-contacts-when-I-popped-them-out pair of glasses. The only pair that's missing? Rose-colored, of course.

I finally whittled down the contents of my purse — it's taken me about 25 years but I figured out all you really, truly need is a phone, ID, one credit card, keys, one single tissue and a tube of tinted lip balm — to fit into a cute, little clutch and now I have to upsize to an oversized weekender just to accommodate my spectacles. So unfair.

But if you force me to get philosophical about my insane eyesight, I'd say that while I'm having a harder time with my actual vision, other more important things are coming into focus. I should just enjoy having more opportunities to accessorize with chic eyewear. And giant purses.

Truth: As kids, we eat Rice Krispies. As adults, we sound like them: snap, crackle, pop.

My Nobel Prize Speech

The following is the acceptance speech I plan to deliver to the Nobel Prize ceremonies in Sweden when I am awarded the Nobel Prize in Physiology or Medicine for my discovery that mothering children can, in fact, render you to be completely and chronically tired for the rest of your life. This condition is known as Chronic Matigue Syndrome (CMS), sometimes called mommyalgic encephalomyelitis (ME):

(Raucous applause)

"Thank you, thank you all very much. I have to say, I never expected to be standing before you today and it is such an incredible honor to be here before the likes of... Bob? Bob Dylan? Is that you? You came to THIS ceremony? That is so awesome. Wow, the times they are a-changing..."

(Pause for laughter)

"As someone who picked her major based on the fact that it required only one math class and whose microbiology lab partner banned her from handling test tubes for breaking so many, I never thought I'd be receiving this award for discovering and identifying the insidious disease known as Chronic Matigue Syndrome.

"It's a debilitating disorder, characterized by profound fatigue, sleep abnormalities, pain, supreme periods of fogginess…and…and…one more thing…Oh, yes! Forgetfulness! You can't imagine what it's like to get a phone call from school, the shame you feel, because you've forgotten to pick up one of your children. In fact, you plain forgot you had that third kid. It's horrible. And, I know because I'm more than just the person who discovered this disease…I am also a sufferer…

(Gasps from the crowd)

"I remember the first time I went to my doctor, complaining of being tired all the time and falling asleep in the middle of the afternoon at work. At home, on the couch, I'd start nodding off at 8 p.m. even when one of my favorite TV shows was on. My bloodwork was normal, no thyroid abnormalities, nothing.

"My doctor said it was no surprise to be wiped out. She reminded me that I had three kids and a job — which immediately threw me into a panic because I'd only been packing lunches for two and hadn't gone into the office in two weeks. She actually wrote me a prescription for a daily nap. But I never filled it. Never felt like I could.

(Sighs and sympathetic tongue clicks reverberate throughout the auditorium)

"A few years later, I was back complaining of the same symptoms. She checked me over, did more bloodwork — which showed normal levels of all the gooey internal stuff — and told me again it wasn't surprising, given my lifestyle.

"I went out into the community and started sharing my story and do you know what I found? I was not alone. In the course of my research — conducted at work, meetings, sidelines of sports practices — other women, all mothers, reported having the same, exact symptoms. There's an entire population suffering.

"The struggle is real. Chronic matigue syndrome is real. Acknowledgment of the disease is step one. Now, we need to focus on a cure because there isn't one. Yet. The most commonly prescribed course of treatment — a solo trip to the Bahamas — is pricey and not often covered by insurance...

(Disbelieving murmurs)

"And, the truth is, it's just a Band-Aid. You may be in the Bahamas, but you're still a mom, you're still worrying about your family back at home. Plus, the internet still works there; the kids can still text you, asking where do you keep the glue sticks? How do you run the washing machine again? Motherhood is a very demanding job and one from which you never really, truly get a paid vacation.

"So, we soldier on. But not in silence. Let's go forward and from now on, don't be afraid to ask for help. Ask a kid to set the table, ask a kid to help with chores, and yeah, they'll probably ignore you but maybe not if we add a hashtag and throw this movement onto social media.

"All it takes is a bunch of moms, posting selfies on Instagram, bags under their eyes on full display, with some catchy hashtag. Let's make a difference. Let's get some help. Now. And never, ever forget
— #PickupyourcrapalreadyandleavemealonesoIcantakeana pforChrissake."

(Standing ovation — of course.)

Vocabulary Word: *evacuumate* (v) When the dogs flee because the vacuum's running.

Would You Like a Side of Fries with Your Order?

Slowly but surely, it happens.

It's just a matter of time.

At first, you sneak a quick glance. But it soon progresses — to full-blown reading.

Before you know it, you're flipping ahead to the obits and, worse, you start to recognize the names and faces.

Man, getting older…

Just like shit, it happens.

Such a privilege and yet also such a pain in the neck…and knees…and lower back, among other places.

Before you know it, every passing birthday triggers a midlife crisis. Although, to be honest, every birthday since I turned 21 has resulted in midlife-crisis soul searching. What am I doing with my life? What is my legacy? What does it all mean? Of course, a midlife crisis in your 20s is wildly different from one in your 40s, which is full-on legit.

But, whoever thinks they're going to grow up and be 40 one day? No 11-year-old ever.

When I was that age, we had these things called board games because we didn't have home computers or cell phones, but we did have cardboard. And imagination. I adored The Game of Life. I felt so grownup when I played it.

I got to make decisions about college, work, my family. I was in charge of all my little plastic pegs and pieces.

Pretty heady stuff for someone still wearing braces.

I couldn't wait to grow up.

Ta da! Now I am! To be honest, I'd kinda like to go back in time and bitch-slap my 11-year-old self for not appreciating how good I had it. Someone drove me everywhere, cooked for me, did my laundry. Sigh. I miss that.

Here I am in my 40s, mother of three, discovering stray white hairs in places I didn't think possible, driving a minivan — which from today forward I shall refer to as a "party wagon" and now let's see how many parents want me to shuttle their middle schoolers to soccer — and thinking more and more about what kind of impact I will leave on the world beyond my carbon, size-7 footprint. Mind-blowing.

I don't play Life any more, I live it.

None of my kids has even heard of this game. My family's party game of choice is Quiplash. It can be played on phones and tablets, which automatically gained favor with the kids. It's wildly entertaining and since three out of three children adore being recognized as quick-witted, it's mostly enjoyed by all. I'm constantly amused by the kids' cleverness. It's stunning how quickly those minds can work because their neurons never seem to be fully firing properly when it comes time to find the container of milk directly in front of them or remember to bring their important homework to school the next day even though it's right by the door where it was strategically left the night before.

One evening, during a rousing round of Quiplash, the task that came up was to create a caption for a tombstone. No. 3, who's not even old enough to work in fast food, typed "Order up."

This made us all laugh hysterically. And then that night, while I was still chuckling over it, I realized, oh crap, that really does sum up life.

If my order was, indeed, up tomorrow, what have I done?

Gulp.

It triggered a fresh midlife crisis. And, it wasn't even my birthday.

To recap: I went to my safety school, the college that offered full tuition and was right in my backyard. I didn't take a chance by going to the little California school that repeatedly sent a recruiter to my high school to sway me to enroll. While working my way through a journalism degree, I accepted an internship in my hometown rather than striking out for Pennsylvania, a state I'd never even been to, to copy edit, which I'd never done before. I kept working for the same newspaper that offered me that internship and ended up sticking around for 26 years. I covered adrenalin-pumping stuff like drive-by shootings and homicides, but it was the quiet stories, the personality profiles that I loved. I adored talking to people and digging into their lives.

No, I never nabbed a Pulitzer Prize, but I did get some awards and sometimes even the nice, occasional email. It was good until it wasn't.

As I mentioned many, many pages earlier (on maybe even just the second page) I watched my oldest child visiting colleges and swinging for the fences, putting herself out there and applying to top colleges. I kept telling her to take chances, but I wasn't exactly following my own advice. Then, I decided to be brave. Take a chance. Quit.

I wrote a resignation letter, longer than some of my newspaper articles, and spilled out my guts, apparently in pale-blue font because technology is not my friend, to the big wigs. In a very Jerry Maguire move, I posted my "mission statement" on Facebook.

The response floored me. It didn't go quite viral, but definitely bacterial — nearly 500 people took the time to have some sort of emoji reaction. Hundreds wrote lovely, heartfelt notes. Strangers, people I'd interviewed, a former journalism professor, coworkers, faithful readers.

To put that in perspective, I might get a few responses to something I'd post, maybe six if it was an especially cute picture of my fluffy little dog.

The outpouring was amazing. Overwhelming. I felt like I attended my own funeral. And, it was pretty awesome. I'm not sure exactly how it would work, but everyone should figure out a way to attend his or her own wake. It's life-affirming in the ultimate, Sally Field kind of way: You like me! You really like me!

My resignation letter even was published in the Columbia Journalism Review. I kind of love the irony that I spent more than half my life in journalism and was recognized by the Review only after I got jumped out of the biz.

In newspapers, probably in most industries, you don't get a lot of feedback. You write a story, send it along to an editor and that's that. Cue the sound of crickets chirping in the hot, still night. Unless you really rile readers. Which can happen.

There were a few stories well, most of them, that really only mattered to the one person featured and that was always enough for me because I'm one of those people who believes in the Starfish Effect. You know, that old story about the kid trying to rescue starfish? Of course you do, everyone does. Isn't there even a Lifetime movie?

Pretty sure every kid around fifth grade has to learn that tale in the hopes of getting those self-involved little turds to think about someone other than themselves for a change.

So anyway, in the starfish story a little kid — sometimes it's a girl and sometimes a boy — goes to the beach and finds all these starfish washed up on the sand and starts tossing them, one by one, back into the ocean. A man watches the scene unfold, and, being a jerk, asks the kid why bother since he/she can't save them all?

"You can't possibly make a difference," Mr. Jackass says.

"I made a difference to that one," the child answers back.

Mic drop.

And really, isn't that all any of us can do? Make a difference in any way we can to anyone we can? We can't all go out and create a nonprofit that's going to end world hunger, but if we make a point of regularly donating to the local food bank, we help families in the most basic, important way. It just takes one seemingly small move. The ripple effect. Ya gotta believe it.

I do.

Early in my reporting career, a call was transferred to my extension. It was a 14-year-old girl. I don't know why she called the newspaper of all places, but she did. Her sad story tumbled out in a flood. Her dad had died and she was shipped off to her unfit mother, an addict. This poor kid wasn't enrolled in school, had run away, gotten pregnant, miscarried, run away again and was absolutely lost.

I didn't have any answers, but I knew where to find them.

"Let me help you, let me make some calls," I told her.

She wouldn't leave a number but promised to call me back.

I dialed around to Child Protective Services and other agencies, stockpiling info and then I waited.

And waited. And waited.

She didn't call.

Weeks passed. I tucked the notes away on my desk, but kept them close, just in case. I thought about that kid a lot. I even wrote a column that ran three months after she first dialed. Guess what? She finally called. She was so excited.

"That story was about me!" she said.

Pretty surprising, right? Someone under 60 read the paper.

I gave her all the info I'd gathered and wished her the best.

It was one story that made a difference to one person. At least, that's what I hope. I don't know whatever happened, but I choose to believe she turned her life around.

I must believe that.

What's the meaning of life? I dunno. I didn't get a perfect 1600 on the SAT, I can't do math unless it's something critical, like figuring out 30 percent off the sale price. But, I do know that I have not one, but three starfish in my hands and I'm trying to make a difference for them and I feel pretty darn good about that if that's my only legacy.

So, fine, order up.

Here it is: my resignation letter. In case you missed it on Facebook or in the, cough, cough, Columbia Journalism Review.

So this is it. I'm done.

After 26 years at the Arizona Daily Star, I'm hanging up my media badge.

If I come up and ask you something that seems incredibly nosy, that's all on me now. Sheer snoopiness. I no longer can hide behind a reporter's right to know.

It's been fun, it's been frustrating. It's been long. The time is right to check out of the newspaper biz.

I've always joked that I — the one who worked part time and received no benefits or raises — would be the last one left, the one who'd turn out the newsroom lights, just like I turned them on for so many years when, as part of juggling parenthood and paycheck, I'd adjusted my shift to start at 6:30 in the a of m.

I've covered the worst of the worst. Murders, homicide trials, stories so shockingly awful they still haunt me. One of my mementos is a small, color photo of a young teen, lips painted red, holding a basketball on her lap and a trophy in the other hand. This 15-year-old girl went to a sleepover, gave birth to a baby in a toilet and strangled him.

Tragic on so many levels. Covering that case landed me on a cross-country flight to New York for a spot on a daytime talk show. The hot topic was the epidemic of teen pregnancy. The show taped on the very same set as "Saturday Night Live." While waiting to go on air, I sat on Cheri Oteri's lightly soiled, green couch, feeling just nervous enough to make a stain of my own on the well-worn fabric.

I've hunted for rattlesnakes and sweet-talked a James Beard-award winning chef into letting me feed him fried Spam and watermelon. I wrote about the woman who makes treats for the animals at the zoo, hydroplaned on the very track used to train police officers and firetruck drivers and hung out with the 4-year-old lead singer of his family's rock band. Little dude wrote his own songs including one that used the word "meow" 16 times. The song, of course, was called "Cowboy Kitty."

Hardboiled types dismiss the stuff I've written (and loved the most) as unimportant "fluff." But that fluff — the little piece about the 72-year-old woman who took up stilt walking — is the stuff that ends up carefully cut out and saved in a box of family treasures. "Remember when grandma was in the paper?" Being on the front page is something special that not many can brag about.

It's a huge responsibility to be trusted to tell someone's story.

When you write a feature, you're invited in. You hear dark secrets, great joys. You laugh with strangers, cry with them. A few hours later, you're friends.

And the feature stories that come from these interviews are just what people need — more than ever — after wading through headline after headline of gloom and doom. Fluff? No, it's the writing equivalent of a warm blanket, a steaming cup of cocoa that soothes as the storm rages outside.

But newspapers are struggling. The staffs are shrinking, just like the paper itself. Sometimes, I spot the flat, plastic-wrapped package on my driveway and it's hard to tell if it's really the paper or a "Find Jesus" pamphlet. There are still plenty of stories to tell, but fewer people to tell them. And fewer people who want to pay to read them.

It is what it is.

Bless those Spotlighters out there who are still fighting the good fight. I love hearing about the small, family-run papers making a difference in their communities. I don't love that many newspapers are run by corporations with policies to reward their CEOs with six-figure raises while laying off the foot soldiers who've been faithfully toiling in the trenches. I think it sucks that newsrooms are full of idealistic people who work hard because they believe in what they do and because they want to highlight injustice and yet they're not valued or appropriately compensated. More than once a coworker was laid off only to be hired back a year or so later to the same job — for less money. Most journalists sure as heck aren't in the field for any monetary reward. They do it because ink runs through their veins.

I have, well, had coworkers who revel in hate mail. I wish I could be as thick-skinned. Instead, I kept a "validation" folder. I treasure those notes from readers who would take the time to tell me they liked something bearing my byline. Sometimes they would tell me a story back. It's a special connection to have someone you've never met feel like they can talk to you.

Those faithful subscribers are the ones who kept me going. But, I've done all I can with this medium.

I cringe when I read the paper and see simple grammatical errors or careless mistakes like two versions of the same story running in different sections. But, I get how it happens. There's less time and fewer eyes to catch goofs. I don't judge. Mistakes happen. We're human.

I'm human.

And so I see my 17-year-old daughter, who's got the world at her fingertips, exploring colleges. It's scary, but mostly it's exciting. Limitless. The world is never more full of possibilities than when you're 17. Maybe even when you're 47.

I'm not too old to make a change.

What is it I want to do? What I wanted to do when I was 7: write a book. Although now I would not write about a white horse with a gleaming silver mane.

I think I can pull this off. After all, I have pinky-swears from two people who said they'd buy any book I wrote. So, that's two sales.

When my middle child was in kindergarten, she sang a song called "Kindergarten Blues" for a talent show. It was, as you can guess, all about the hardship and suckiness of that initial foray into school. But, the triumphant last line — and one she performed with a giant smile and happily jiggling jazz hands — is "A girl's gotta do what a girl's gotta do."

That's how I feel.

You can't see it, but my hands are waving.

Oh yeeeeeeeeaaaaaaaaah.

RIP...Me

Backstory: A friend shared a library-sponsored event called "Write Your Own Obituary — It's About Life!" He thought I'd want to write about it and he was correct. What a great idea. Aside from the intriguing topic, I'm down with anything that involves an exclamation point. It must be good! Sadly, the seminar died an untimely death — the event was canceled before it ever happened.

But, having written plenty of obituaries for other people, I figured I probably had the chops to tackle my own. Plus, I'm enough of a control freak to doubt someone else will get it right. So, here goes:

COOK, Kristen, age 99, of Tucson, Ariz., died at home in her massive walk-in closet, which was so filled to capacity with shoes that the shelves buckled, crushing her instantly. She died with a smile on her face, surrounded by what she loved most: her shoes.

Relax, kids — that said WHAT she loved most. WHOM she loved most was obviously you guys and your dad. Sheesh.

Cook was the ultimate multihyphenate — wife, mother, writer, swagger coach*, cook (which is confusing because it's her last name but she was also quite the culinary artiste — except for that one time she made roasted beets, which everyone hated, oh and the brownies with no sugar), dog-lover, lifelong minivan driver, shopper extraordinaire, shoe-hoarder and diehard "30 Rock" fan.

Born in Jacksonville, Ark., she lived a few years in Guam before her parents uprooted her and her younger brother to Tucson, which, from what she'd heard from other people, was a scary desert place with rattlesnakes. From ages 6-8, she refused to completely stretch out her body in her twin bed, lest her feet be too close to the edge, which is where she was convinced rattlesnakes were hiding beneath the covers, coiled and waiting to strike.

She tried her best to be a good person and to be considerate of others — except for that stretch in middle school when getting kicked out of the library with her

---

* I don't really know what a swagger coach is, but Tom Haverford described himself as one on "Parks and Recreation" and I really liked the sound of it.

besties for being too loud happened every day school was in session. She showed her appreciation through baked goods, usually cookies. She loved to laugh and make others laugh and while people secretly hated her for getting carded well into her 70s, she graciously shared her tips for youthful, glowing skin, which included never refusing a piece of chocolate and using coconut oil to smear the makeup off her face.

Her biggest regret in life was cheaping out and not paying the $70 asking price on the gorgeous, green silk with zipper detail, floor-length Alexander Wang maxi dress listed on Poshmark in 2015. Oh, and Cook did also feel bad about the time she tricked her science teacher into trying a bite of a bean and cheese burrito she'd forgotten in her locker over Christmas break. Sorry, Mr. Carpenter.

Her most difficult life experience was not the unintentional natural childbirth of her third baby but rather the process of writing her first book, which required her to make the ballsy move of quitting the only job at the only place she'd ever worked as an adult. It was fun and difficult and while she was, eventually, glad and proud that she endured the amazingly soul-sucking process of trying to publish her first book, she was most proud of her children. Cook delighted in telling people about their accomplishments — one snared a Nobel prize for bettering the world through computer science, while another earned a record-breaking 20 NBA MVP awards and then one has the distinction of being the most-watched YouTube celebrity to crash the internet. Twice.

In lieu of flowers, the family asks that people donate generously to charities and to do one small, thoughtful thing for someone, whether it's paying a stranger a compliment or scheduling an appointment to donate blood.

Her last request was that friends and family attend her memorial service in their most fabulous pair of shoes.

No Crocs allowed.

---30---

31762393R00163

Made in the USA
San Bernardino, CA
08 April 2019